Feeding the Flame:

Honoring Loki, Sigyn and Their Family

Galina Krasskova

Feeding the Flame

Honoring Loki, Sigyn, and Their Family

Compiled by Galina Krasskova

Asphodel Press

Hubbardston, Massachusetts

Asphodel Press
12 Simond Hill Road
Hubbardston, MA 01452

Feeding the Flame
© 2008 Galina Krasskova
ISBN 978-0-6152-0761-2

Printed in cooperation with
Lulu Enterprises, Inc.
860 Aviation Parkway, Suite 300
Morrisville, NC 27560

Because I promised this long ago, Loki, for You,
for Sigyn and for Your family.

And because I love You both.

Acknowledgements

Many thanks to all those who lovingly submitted the works of their hands and hearts: the poetry, recipes, invocations, prayers and writing out of love, respect and devotion to Loki and His family. This devotional is an offering of love and joy. May it please Them.

A special thanks to both Grace Palmer and Mordant Carnival, for designing a beautiful cover, and also to Joshua Tenpenny, formatter and computer genius extraordinaire.

Thanks to Elizabeth Vongvisith who gave me the title for this devotional.

And as always, I offer thanks both to Fuensanta Arismendi (Plaza), who more than anyone else, has taught me about humility and devotion to the Gods, especially Sigyn; and to Raven Kaldera, Hel's shaman and a very patient mentor to a very stubborn Odin's woman.

I could never have compiled this offering without your collective help.

Contents

Introduction 1

Hot Stuff: Working with Loki 4

Loki 30

Honor to Loki 31

Tale of the Anti-Hero 32

Contemplating A Tour 34

Fulltrui 35

Untitled 38

An Orchestra in Twenty-Six Parts 39

Invocation to Loki 41

Loki 42

My Beloved Conundrum 43

Courting the Trickster 44

Trickster 48

For Loki 50

Drop Dead Loki 52

Full Cycle 57

Sigyn: Loki's Gentle Bride 59

Prayer to Sigyn 64

Sigyn Blessing Oil 65

Sigyn's Song 66

Victory 69

Sigyn's Courage 72

Ah, Sigyn 76

Visiting Sigyn 78

Sigyn's Angst 81

Sigyn's Lesson 83

Sigyn Bath 86

Resolve 87

Eaten Whole 88

Loki and Sigyn's First Meeting 89

Violet 97

Stand By Your Man (as told by Sigyn)..........................99
Invocation to Sigyn...109
A Meditation on Sigyn's Bowl..................................110
Daily Meditation for Loki and Sigyn 112
In the Cave...115
Sigyn: More Than Words...118
A Group Ritual To Honor Sigyn 124
Words Given To A Devotee by Narvi and Vali...........129
Prayer to Narvi and Vali 130
Lament for Narvi..131
For Vali...133
Wergild..135
Grieving for Narvi..138
Three Wishes..140
Vali 142
Two Prayers and an Offering.....................................142
Joy 144
Sleipnir: Noblest of Steeds 146
Steel..148
First 150
Hag of the Iron Wood 152
Angrboda Incense...154
Two for Angrboda..155
Angrboda, Mistress of the Ironwood 157
The Hag As Mother..159
For Glut, from Her First Husband 164
Jormundgand's Breath..166
Jormungandr 167
Oh Jormungand..168
Third Snake 170
The Binding Ones...172
Mother of Monsters..174
For Fenris 178
Learning to Love the Wolf...180

The Killer's God 182

A Prayer of Gratitude 185

For the Hel of It 187

For Hel On Walpurgisnacht 188

Darkness Out Of Fire 190

Loki the Fool 192

About the Author *194*

Other Books by Galina Krasskova *195*

Introduction

Compiling this devotional has been a joyous and often wrenching process. On the one hand, I found beautiful, powerful and heart-felt submissions pouring in not only for Loki and Sigyn but for Their children as well. On the other, in allowing Loki and Sigyn to guide this project (as indeed was Their right to do), I was at times confronted with terrible, painful and occasionally shattering truths about Them, such as the enormity and rawness of Sigyn's grief over the loss of Her sons. None of this was easy, yet it is my hope that the final product, the work of so many hearts and hands, will prove a worthy offering to the Gods we love so dearly. It is my hope that it will help people who wish to honor these Gods, and for whom so very little in the form of prayers or rituals currently exists. And we do love Them. That truth, more than any other, lies at the heart of this devotional. It is an offering of love and adoration to Gods who are all too often forgotten, maligned or relegated to the shadows of common worship, as though we humans had the right to determine which Gods are and are not *worthy* of honor, we in our hubris.

When I began this book, I had planned only to include material about Loki and Sigyn Themselves. As I progressed however, I rapidly came to realize that there was no way I could do that. Their story is bound up inextricably with that of Their children, and in Loki's case, with His other partners. I could not separate the various interlocking threads and relationships without, in my eyes, doing these Gods a grave injustice (and enough injustice has been done Them). Therefore, dear Reader, you will find prayers and poetry to or about Angrboda, Odin, Glut, Eisa, Einmyrja, Fenris, Jormungand, Narvi and Vali, Hela and even Sleipnir. The first three are intimately connected to Loki and the others are His children, each worthy of honor in His or Her own right but honored here as part of a loving family.

As I write this, worshipping Loki and His family remains very controversial within modern Heathenry. There are those who love these Gods dearly, but fear to speak of that devotion lest they lose the fragile net of their religious community. There are certain denominations of Heathenry in which even to speak Loki's name is considered dangerous, unlucky and wrong. In online forums and public debate, I have seen these divine beings slandered and mocked, cursed and dismissed, and in every case approached with a superstitious fear and dread that belies Their holy nature. Whether or not to honor Loki and His kin has become one of the major ideological faultlines within this modern body of religions, and that does not appear to be changing any time soon. So, as Mordant Carnival said to me after an intense experience with Loki October 2007: "To those who will not speak Loki's name, I say good! It is a holy name. They don't have the right to speak it!"

To those who love and gladly hail Loki and His family, it is my wish that this devotional will be of use to you. These prayers, poems, rituals, and recipes were collected from around the world from people who have long cherished the wisdom this particular family of Gods has to share. May these words serve to open the hearts of those who read them to these Gods and to Their kin.

When I first published *The Whisperings of Woden* three years ago, there were no other devotionals extant within either Heathenry or Norse Paganism. Today, just within the past year, that has changed and dramatically so. Thanks in part to Asphodel Press, we now have not only my own devotionals but Elizabeth Vongvisith's beautiful paean to Loki, *Trickster, My Beloved*, as well as her devotional poetry collection *Love and Shadows*. (Asphodel Press itself has published an extensive collection of rituals and prayers titled *The Pagan Book of Hours*.) There is a forthcoming devotional to Frey, one to Hela, and another Loki devotional by Tracy Nichols—*From The Heart, For The Heart*. Outside of Asphodel Press, there are devotionals to Frigga and to Saga in progress, and I recently heard rumors of one to Thor. Best of all, this outpouring of devotional consciousness is affecting not only Heathenry but also Hellenismos, which is seeing the first devotional to Artemis published later this year (*Dancing in Moonlight* by Thista

Minai) and Kemetic (Egyptian) Paganism, which will see the publication of a devotional to Sekhmet in 2008. This is a joyous thing, not only for the Gods but for our communities, which have long underestimated the need and value of such interior practices.

It is my sincere hope that soon we shall have devotionals in print to every single one of our Gods and Goddesses, as daunting a prospect as this might seem! Each heart turned to Them in love and devotion, after all, is a window to the world through which those Deities can act. And that, to this author at least, is a joy beyond imagining.

GALINA KRASSKOVA
NOVEMBER 15, 2007
NEW YORK CITY

Hot Stuff: Working with Loki
Mordant Carnival

Part 1: Meet the Man with the Tattered Smile

> *There is one tallied among the Æsir, whom some call the strife-bearing Ás and the most seductive-speaking, and a blemish on all gods and men. This one is named Loki or Lopt...*
>
> —Gylfaginning (translated by Selvarv Stigard)

> *How shall Loki be known? Thus, to call him son of Farbauti and Laufey and Nál, brother of Býleist and Helblind, father of Vonargand who is Fenris-wolf, and of Jörmungand who is the Miðgarð-wyrm, and Hel and Nari and Ali, kinsman and relative, companion and bench-mate of Óðin and the Æsir, guest and casket-decoration of Geirröð, thief from etins, of goats and Brísingamen and Iðun's apples; Sleipnir's kin; Sigyn's man, enemy of gods, Sif's barber, bale-smith, the sly Ás, insulter and debaser of the gods, Baldr's rede-bane, the bound Ás, defiant enemy of Heimdall and Skaði.*
>
> —Skáldskaparmál (translated by Selvarv Stigard)

> *Loki Loves Me . . . Oh Crap.*
>
> —Bumper sticker

Introduction

This article is not so much for the already fully-functioning Loki-worshipper as for the person who, for whatever reason, finds him or herself needing to get some basic information on how to approach the Son of Laufey. Maybe He's always interested you; maybe you're getting spooky little pokes to go and have a chat; maybe He stars as the villain in your new comic and you want to keep Him sweet.

You will notice that Loki is dealt with as if He were literally real. That's because as far as I'm concerned, Loki is as real as the Prime Minister. If you need a nice cosy piece that talks comfortingly of god-forms and archetypes, or discusses deities as if They were consumer goods that you can pick up and put down at your convenience, you will have to look elsewhere. This is Big God Magic. It involves dealing with

Gods as living consciousnesses with Their own drives, attitudes and agendas that may or may not accord with what you want; independent beings that can walk into your dreams demanding cigarettes and coffee, drag you out of bed for a walk at four in the morning to look at an interesting bit of graffiti, make you burst out laughing in the middle of the supermarket, and quite possibly turn your entire life upside down.

Although I'm writing from a Heathen perspective, this piece is aimed at magicians in general. I've tried to keep things loose and undogmatic, since Loki is well-known for dropping in on people from other traditions, or no trad at all for that matter. The working described contains Heathen elements, but is not a reconstructionist working. In any case, it is impossible to reconstruct an authentic pre-Christian rite to Loki, as no such thing was ever recorded. (I should point out, though, that like any God it is far better to approach Loki having informed yourself of His historical and cultural context. If you can't be bothered to read a few texts, you should probably stick to evoking Pokemon.)

Whilst it's better to look to the extant lore to understand these Gods, what has come down to us was written by Christians and not people who actually worshipped Them. Therefore there are a number of influences and interpolations that need to be processed and sieved through, and interpretations are likely to vary from one group or individual to another. This is a fairly personal work drawn from my own experiences as well as from lore; it should be reasonably clear to the reader what's lore-based and what is derived from experience or some other inspiration (unsubstantiated personal gnosis, or UPG).

The Trickster

There's something about trickster Gods in general that puts the wind up people, and few have worse press than Loki. The hysteria is bad enough amongst magicians and Neo-Pagans generally. It's even worse amongst people who worship the Northern pantheon full-time, some of whom won't even speak or write Loki's name. Partly to blame is the notable inability of certain modern authors to use the T-word without some bludgeoning adjective (you're never just a Trickster, you're a malicious Trickster, or an evil Trickster); that, and lazy attempts to shoehorn the pantheon into an ill-fitting Christian model with Odin as a rough approximation of God, Baldr as processed Jesus-flavoured deity product and Loki as Satan.

However, Trickster figures in general are not evil, dangerous critters to be avoided at all costs. They are holy, necessary, having special virtues that 'safer' Gods do not. To imagine that one can sort out which are the nice safe Gods and spirits and work exclusively with them is a mistaken idea. Loki is not Satan, any more than Odin is Jehovah. Far from being a figure of unadulterated evil, a quick glance at the Eddas tells us that Loki has provided the Æsir with many of Their best toys, including Thor's hammer and Odin's magical spear. He wins valuable allies and resolves dangerous situations—although, granted, a lot of these are of His own making.

God or Giant?

Another reason offered as to why one should not work with or venerate Loki is that Loki is not a God. He is dismissed variously as an hypostasis (an independent sub-personality) of Odin, a plot device created by Snorri Sturlusson, and as a 'Giant' who has somehow inveigled His way into Asgard (what, did He lie about His height?). It's true that Loki is a full-blooded Jötun, but so are several other Gods and Goddesses, and most Æsir have at least one Jötun parent. Besides which, the Eddas refer to Loki as a member of the Æsir several times. In fact, the term 'Giant' as a translation of Jötun is rather unhelpful altogether—it is better to conceive of the Jötnar (singular Jötun, feminine Jötynja) as a separate but related tribe of Gods, rather than a hostile and chaotic race apart.

It's also brought up ad nauseam that there is no historical evidence for the worship of Loki. In fact, it would be more accurate to say that there is no conclusive evidence; however, there are tantalising hints, such as various place-names that seem to derive from Loki's name and records of people having Loki as a byname (although this probably did not refer to the God). Men in Iceland are still christened Lopt, a heiti of Loki's. The Icelandic name for the star Sirius is Lokabrenna, often translated as Loki's Brand. There are also a number of old folk sayings recorded that refer to Loki: hopelessly tangled thread was "something for Loki to mend His trousers with," and when the fire flared up and threw off sparks, people in Scandinavia once used to say that Loki was beating His children. The skin from a pan of boiling milk might also be thrown into the flames as a sort of offering to Loki. Shimmering atmospheric effects were attributed to "the Loki-man" sowing His oats or driving His goats to pasture. (It's unclear whether the Loki these terms refer to is precisely the same Loki as the God, of course. The name seems to be used in pretty much the same way that 'fairy' is used in other parts of Europe, to indicate something that is inexplicable, irksome, or not what it appears to be.) There also exists a Faroese ballad, collected in the 18th century but probably far older, where a family menaced by an evil giant pray to Odin, Hoenir and Loki and are saved when the latter tricks and kills the giant. The story ends with Loki and the family in a group hug.

Fire

Something else that gets kicked around a lot is the identification of Loki with the element of fire. It is true that this may not have been a part of His character as described by Snorri, and that the name Loki and the word for fire may not be etymologically related as some have speculated. However, some evidence exists to connect Loki with fire. Several of the aforementioned folk-sayings mention fire, and the association with Sirius seems to imply a connection with heat and flame. There also exists a carved stone bellows-shield from Jutland, featuring a male face with stitched-shut lips—an attribute of Loki's. (The Dick Dastardly moustache sported by the carving, not so much.) My personal response to the question of whether or not Loki used to be a fire-God a thousand years ago is an exasperated "Well, He is *now*." I've seen and experienced too many odd fire-related phenomena in respect of my work with Loki to ignore.

Shape-Shifter, Sex-Changer

Loki is a noted shapeshifter. In the legends, we see Him transform several times: into a horse, into a fly, into a salmon and into a falcon. This last is interesting, because it seems that Loki can't change into a bird under His own steam—the only times we see Him in bird-form are when Freyja lends Him Her magical falcon cloak. He possesses a pair of magical shoes that let Him run through the air, but they don't seem to get Him very far—when we see Him use them to elude pursuit He's easily fetched back by Thor. For long journeys between Asgard and Jötunheim, Loki appears to require Freyja's aid. This seems significant. It has been pointed out by various scholars that the donning of animal disguises is associated with various shamanic practices, as indeed is transvestitism, so it seems reasonable to infer that the stories of Loki and the falcon-dress may allude to such practices.

Loki seems to make rather a habit of wearing women's clothing. In the Lay of Thrym, Loki dresses as a bridesmaid to aid Thor (disguised as Freyja and monumentally annoyed about it) in journeying to Jötunheim to retrieve His stolen hammer, Mjollnir. Elsewhere we see Him go one better; not only does He shapeshift into a mare, but he has sex with a stallion and falls pregnant with Sleipnir, Odin's magical eight-legged steed. There's a tantalizing reference in *Lokasenna* to Loki's having spent eight years under the earth, bearing children and apparently lactating—He is accused of having given milk "like a cow and a woman." There's also a line in the Lesser Voluspa describing how Loki consumed the heart of the witch Gullveig, thrice-burned by the Æsir yet still living, and became magically pregnant from it, giving birth to a brood of *flagð* (female witches and monsters). Another important point to note is that Loki's surname is Laufeyarsson—He's named for His mother, Laufey, not His father, Farbauti.

Loki has also produced offspring in the more normal manner. With His wife Sigyn He had two sons, Vali and Narvi; and with the Jötynja Angrboda He fathered Fenrir, the gigantic ravening wolf prophesied to kill Odin at the end of time, Jormundgand, the great World Serpent, and the death-Goddess Hela.

The Gifts of Loki

As mentioned before, Loki provided the Æsir with some of Their most potent items. This occurred as a direct of Loki's own mischief. It seems that Thor's beloved wife Sif was possessed of a beautiful mane of gleaming golden hair. Loki one day took it into His head to chop it all off while Sif was asleep. Why on earth He did this is not adequately explored, but Kveldulf Gundarsson has speculated that since having the hair shorn was once a punishment for adultery, the act may have been code for Loki seducing her. Whether or not He and Mrs. Hlórriþi got a thing going on, matters could not be made right until the hair had been replaced. Loki therefore went to the Dwarves and got two master craftsmen working against one another, wagering His own head that one couldn't outdo the other. He then turned into a fly and pestered the Dwarf at the forge bellows so the goods would be impaired and He'd win the bet.

Loki returned to Asgard not just with Sif's new hair, a wig of living gold that grew on its own, but with Odin's terrible spear Gungnir that never misses, and the arm-ring Draupnir that makes a new armring every nine nights. He brought Freyr a magic ship, Skidbladnir, that can fit all the armies of Asgard and yet be folded up as small as a napkin, and a mystical golden boar who shone like the sun and could run across the worlds and never get tired. Most famous of all these gifts, of course, was Thor's hammer Mjollnir: unbreakable, guaranteed never to miss its mark, and always to return to Thor's hand. Its only flaw was that it was a little short in the handle, the craftsman's assistant having been distracted by some stinging insect while it was being made.

Loki didn't do so well out of the enterprise. Having lost His bet, He was now confronted by an irate Dwarf looking to collect. Loki barely wriggled out of that one. Loki pointed out that to claim His head, the Dwarf would need to cut through His neck—not part of the deal. The Dwarf was understandably furious at being used as a patsy and proceeded to drill holes in Loki's lips with an awl, then took a thong and stitched His mouth shut tight. Loki had to tear the thong out, and if you meet Him now you will notice that His lips are still scarred.

You will note that He did not keep any of the shiny things for Himself. Loki isn't about hanging onto stuff.

Loki Unbound

According to the Eddas, Loki eventually angered the Æsir so much that They seized Him, took Him to a cave and bound Him over three sharp rocks with the guts of His own son. The Etin-bride Skaði hung a venomous serpent over Loki's head which drips poison down onto His face. His faithful wife Sigyn catches the poison in a bowl, but sometimes She must stop to empty it. Then the poison falls onto Loki's face, and He writhes so hard in His bonds that the Earth shakes. He will never be free until Ragnarök comes, and He sets out to do battle with His mortal foe Heimdall.

People sometimes ask, reasonably enough, how Loki can have dealings with us when He is bound under the earth? There are various explanations. One is that Ragnarök has come and gone. I don't buy this, not least because I've spoken to a lot of the Gods that are supposed to die and they don't act very dead. Two, more sensible, is that Loki is a God and can surely be manifest in more than one place at once. His Mysteries—mischief, chaos, passion, intellect, creativity, destruction—are very much at large in the world; it follows then that the God must be present too.

Another version of events which I've heard from a few people who deal with Him in a religious context is that He was either freed by the Æsir or escaped in some other way, but that His years of binding have damaged Him permanently, driving Him insane. The bound attribute of Loki can therefore be said to exist in Loki's own mind, manifesting as the tortured insanity that He sometimes displays. He will only be completely free of it in death, which more or less fulfils the prophecies as laid down in lore.

Me, I don't know. There are some things I'm not even supposed to think about too hard, let alone pry into. I asked Him about it a few times in the early days, and eventually got told that if I asked Him again I'd find out just how bound He was. Make of that what you will.

The Two-Man Grift (and other dubious associations)

Loki and Odin: The relationship between Loki and Odin is a complex one. Kennings for Loki include "brother of Býleist and Helblindi," both of which are themselves by-names of the Old Man. In *Lokasenna,* Loki is referred to as a wish-son (adopted son) of Odin's, and later in the poem He reminds Odin that They have mingled Their blood and made vows together. Taken together these verses are usually interpreted to mean that Odin and Loki are blood-brothers. Some dispute this. The Loki-bashers point out that this reference occurs only in *Lokasenna,* Býleist and Helblind might be a couple of Jötnar who coincidentally share heiti with Odin, and that in any case Loki has broken His vows so that any such tie becomes null and void. The pro-Loki crew point out that this reference occurs only in *Lokasenna,* and that Loki and Odin generally refer to each other as brothers if you talk to Them. I go with the blood-brother interpretation myself, since the Jötnar who parented Loki and Odin are specifically named in lore and would seem to be different individuals.

Some will tell you that They are mortal foes, that Odin hates Loki for killing Baldr and His various other transgressions, and that Loki hates Odin for binding Him in a cave with His son's guts for unnumbered centuries, that He despises Odin and longs for the day when He will fall at Ragnarök. Others will tell you that they are loyal friends and that neither will hear a bad word about the other.

They're both wrong and both right. From Odin I have witnessed great love and terrible sorrow directed at Loki; from Loki I have witnessed devotion, bitterness, love, and a deep abiding fury, none of which serve to dull or attenuate each other. I can tell you that Loki does not despise Odin; as angry as He is at times, He respects His brother. Odin and Loki are intensely similar in some ways, and very different in others. Loki to me embodies a powerful random element that Odin does not; Odin might seem wild and capricious, but there is method to His madness. At times Loki Himself seems not to know why He does what He does, and it's as if this is a necessary part of His nature, a randomness so complete that not even He can be entirely sure what He'll do next.

Loki is also valuable to Odin in that He can achieve things that Odin cannot achieve without a drastic loss of face. He has no face to keep; His honour is a different kind than that displayed by the other Gods. Roads are open to Him that are not open to others. He can breach social mores and circumvent expectations—for example, when He tricks the builder of Asgard's walls (and conceives Sleipnir into the bargain). In particular, He can do what Odin simply cannot do—dark things that must be done in secrecy, like the killing of Baldr.

Loki and Odin seem to come as a pair. If you start knocking around with one of Them, you can expect to deal with the other sooner or later. Their respective natures are well summed up in this quote from Odin's-man Wayland Skallagrimsson: "Odin is a god of transcendence. I think Loki is also a god of transcendence but not quite the same way. Odin's is directed and purposeful, Loki's is more like tying the self to a chair and kicking it down the stairs, laughing madly all the while."

Loki and Baldr: Baldr, son of Odin and the wise Frigg. Beautiful to look upon, so goodly that in His hall no evil deed can be committed, so wise and just that all abide by His word, a being of light and peace and love. Of all the Gods, He is the brightest, the best ... and one of the deadest, because Loki killed Him.

Baldr was virtually invulnerable thanks to the actions of His divine mother. When He suffered foreboding dreams of His own death, She went from world to world and beseeched promises from all creatures, from the plants and the trees and the rocks that none would harm Her beloved son. After this it became a popular sport to throw deadly missiles at Baldr and watch them bounce off. The only Ás who did not participate was Baldr's brother Hodr, who was blind. Loki was having none of this, however. He took on the guise of an elderly woman, and gleaned from Frigg that she had not asked the mistletoe for its oath because it was so small and young. He found a sprig of mistletoe and fashioned an arrow from it, then persuaded Hodr to join in the game. He guided the blind God's hand, the arrow found its mark, and Baldr was slain.

All of Asgard was hurled into mourning. The Death-Goddess Hela agreed to ransom Baldr out of Hel on one condition: that all things wept for Him. Once again, Frigg rode out. Where She'd got promises before, She now wrung tears. Everything wept for Baldr—even the rocks themselves ... all except one being: a Jötynja named Thekk (Thanks) who said she would shed "only dry tears" for Baldr's death. Therefore He remains in Hel, along with His wife Nanna, who died of grief. After Ragnarök He will emerge once more, to become the leading light of the new pantheon.

Precisely why Loki did this depends on who you ask. Snorri seems to take it as read that Loki is an evil git and does not look further; conservative heathens likewise (I've even seen it suggested amongst the more extreme element that Baldr resisted Loki's advances and got Saint-Sebastianned out of the picture). The pro-Loki crowd have a number of different explanations. The simplest is that being presented with an insoluble problem—how to kill an immortal—Loki just had to solve it. Others suggest that Baldr's invulnerability was a violation of the natural order of things, and would have disrupted the very fabric of the Nine Worlds. My favourite explanation is that the whole thing was a scam. A two-man grift, a conspiracy between Loki and Odin.

According to this version, Baldr was killed to protect Him. Frigg could not obtain oaths from those things not yet created or imagined, and so something might one day have arisen that could harm Baldr when the worlds end and Ragnarök comes. Since Baldr is the embodiment of peace and goodness, those qualities would then be absent from the world to come. This way, Baldr gets to sit out Ragnarök in Hel's gaff and can safely re-emerge once the conflict is done.

(Of course this leaves aside a lot of interesting discussion points, such as questions regarding the accuracy of "mistletoe" as a translation and the fact that the version of events in the *Edda* is very different from the version in *Gesta Danorum*, but we'll be here all night if we get into that mess.)

Loki and Thor: Do not underestimate Thor. There's a reason Loki hangs out with Him. Before the oops-He's-evil *volte face,* these two are often seen travelling together in the Eddas. They complement each other very well—Loki's wild cunning and native wit, and Thor's steadfast nature and physical might. This is not a simplistic brains-and-brawn deal; Loki seems to need Thor to balance out His wildness. In *Lokasenna,* Thor is the only God that can stop Loki's insults and eject Him from the hall. This has led some people to suggest that Thor should be called upon to keep Loki in line.

I disagree strenuously with this concept. It insults both wights. Loki is not a misbehaving child who needs a stern hand to keep Him in line, and Thor should not be treated like some celestial bouncer. However, I would recommend that anyone planning to have dealings with Loki over the long term should attempt to set up a good relationship with the Big Guy too, as He can offer you a sort of grounding force to offset the inevitable craziness that working with Loki will bring to the fore. Thor can help you by being your earth-wire, by helping you to stay in contact with the day-to-day world and its demands.

On a personal note, I really like Thor. Sound guy. Likes Jack Daniels. You should look Him up.

Meet the Family: Be advised that if you take up with Loki you are very likely to have dealings with some of His relatives too, especially His kids. Hela and Her various servants may well show up in your life. Or you may be introduced to Fenrir; Loki sometimes sends people down with offerings for His bound son. Be careful with this, because Loki occasionally sends people down *as* offerings too.

Part 2: Getting down to business
The hows and whys of dealing with Loki

Right, enough lore geekery. What's He like?

I'm going to be speaking largely from personal experience here, and personal experience of things like Gods is always going to be a bit of a sticky subject. Aside from the undeniable fact that this may all be a figment of my imagination, different people relate to Him in very different ways and it seems that my experiences have been rather unusual in many respects.

Loki's nature

If Odin is breath, then Loki is blood. He is the warmth rushing to your cheeks when you blush, He is the glow from a shot of liquor on a cold evening. He is the red mist before your eyes when you rage. He is the pulse that dances in your chest when you see someone you love—and the heat at your groin. He is the heart-fire, leaping along every vein, animating you, warming you, setting you aflame.

Loki is creative. He is the brilliant spark of a new idea, the kick and snap of the intellect as it makes a new connection. He is not the wily general crafting masterful stratagems to be played out over time; Loki's thing is contriving plans on the fly, daring to come up with solutions that no one else would even consider.

Loki is destructive, no doubt. At His wildest He is a calamity, come to tear down all the cherished structures of your life. He'll cheerfully destroy not only material stability—job, home, relationship—but will shatter your very Self without compunction. No matter how precious something is to you, if Loki decides it needs to go then it'll go. It is thanks to Loki that Baldr the Beautiful walks no more amongst the Gods, and will never be ransomed out of Hel; do you really imagine He'd think twice about getting your car repossessed? And He does this not out of malice (although believe me, He's perfectly capable of grinning happily as He tears your world to shreds), but because it needs doing. Loki never seems to take anything you really need, although your estimation of what is needful may be radically different from His.

Loki is playful, absurd, foolish at times, vicious and sharp-tongued at others. Everything from scatological joshing to cutting Wildean witticisms are His. He loves to knock the pretentious off their pedestals, and likewise elevate the unappreciated. Some self-proclaimed Lokeans try to excuse unprovoked rude and abusive behaviour by claiming that they are emulating their God. They aren't. Loki isn't about mindless shit-stirring and cheap, thoughtless slurs. His insults hurt because they are founded in truth. He strips away all the bullshit and leaves you staring at your own flaws without the benefit of any comforting illusions. No "I was provoked," no "she was asking for it," no "it was the beer talking," no "my inner child needs holistic healing and wellness before I can accept responsibility," no bollocks, just what you've done, why you did it and who you are. Your worst, deepest-buried, nastiest stuff, all stripped bare and thrown out there like they were "You've got ketchup down your front." It'll hurt like a bastard, and rest assured that Loki will thoroughly enjoy the process. And in the end you will be better for it. To get an idea of what I mean, you should read the *Lokasenna*, in which Loki harangues several of the major Gods. The accusations contained in the poem are not the empty slurs of a bored wind-up merchant, they're awkward truths that the other Gods might prefer not be discussed in public but which need to be aired from time to time (and which the reader of the poem could benefit from learning).

But to have in your life? Well, sometimes He is this playful trickster figure, a little like Diana Wynne Jones' depiction of Him in *Eight Days Of Luke,* or maybe the eponymous character in the film *Drop Dead Fred.* He's the voice in my head that persuades me to disobey and play up when I really need to, the boyish, giggling presence that pokes me into the toyshop or the swimming pool when I'm down in the dumps. But that's quite rare. Most of the time He's a much darker presence, even threatening; however, one of the things I've learned from Him is that in the context of spirit-work scary isn't the same as bad.

A story that illustrates this fairly well is this one. I've always like drawing and painting, but over the years I've developed a lot of anxiety about my artwork. I'd got so hung up on getting it right, doing it properly, that even picking up a pencil and putting it to a clean white page was enough to make my stomach flip over, my chest tighten, and my fingers cramp up. I'd commit to a week of "just doing it," putting pen to paper for a few minutes every day and building from there, and I'd manage maybe a couple of days at a stretch before my stomachache got the better of me. Then one day Loki showed up in my psychic space and told me, *You're going to learn how to draw.*

I told Him that was impossible. I pointed out that I had failed my A-level. *You're going to learn how to draw.* I told Him I couldn't seem to commit to a regular schedule of practice. *You're going to learn how to draw.* I told Him I just didn't have the skill. *You're going to learn how to draw.* We went back and forth like that over a period of a few days, and then I got *You're going to learn how to draw, or I'm going to break your fingers.*

I realised two things. One, that I was lying to myself about my ability. That if I put my mind to it, I could become at least a competent artist—that if I wanted it, it was there, and all I had to do was buckle down and start working. And two, that if I didn't, He really was going to break my fingers. He'd either arrange an accident for me, or more likely wake up my arthritis and fix me that way. I'd had a bad flare-up in my hands some years previous, bad enough that I needed to get other people to open ring-pulls for me and had trouble sleeping because of the pain. I knew that if I didn't do the work I would find myself in a similar condition again—and I'd still have to draw.

Some months later I realised I was drawing every single day without really thinking about it any more; instead of being a huge source of pain, stress and guilt in my life it's become just something I do, not brilliantly but with slow improvement. Loki will get the best out of you, by hook or by crook.

Loki the Father (and Mother)

One thing you should remember when working with Loki is that He loves all His kids. No matter how monstrous they might look to mortal eyes, He loves them. Even the alien chaos of Jormundgand and the ravening Fenrir are beloved; as for the terrifying half-rotted Death Goddess Hela, a nickname for Her amongst Loki's people is "Daddy's Little Princess." If He should adopt you as one of His children, He will love even those parts of you which are monstrous.

Occupational hazards

All the usual hazards of deity-work apply to Loki, as well as a few extra.

Destruction: Before you start approaching Loki, tie up any loose ends. If there's anything you should have done and haven't, do it now. Your car's been making a funny noise all week? Take it to the garage. Haven't backed up your PC for a while? Get on it. This especially includes things you've been hiding from people who might reasonably expect to know about them. Your wife is going to find your lingerie collection, your husband is going to find your porn stash, your boyfriend is going to find out about your other boyfriend and the kids are going to find out what really happened to the dog. If there is anything in your life that can go pear-shaped, assume that it will. If Loki decides to trash your life, then it'll get trashed, but there's no need to give Him an excuse.

Anger and sorrow: Never insult any of Loki's kin. Be aware that promiscuity notwithstanding He loves both Sigyn and Angrboda and will not be impressed if you impugn Them. Angrboda is not a cartoon battleaxe that He sneaks around on and Sigyn is not a patsy. Be very careful how you talk about Loki's children in front of Him; feel free to use kennings for Loki that "namecheck" them in an initial evocatory speech, but once He's manifested, exercise caution. He grieves especially for dead Narvi and bound Fenrir. You might want to avoid the topic altogether until you're ready to minister to His grief or deal with His rage. He is very fond of Hela.

Do not bring up Ragnarök unless He does. "Is [insert current event here] a sign of Ragnarök?" is an especially bad question to ask, because it's not only painful to Him but smacks of hubris—"my generation is special, our disasters are more disastrous and our significance is greater." Every generation thinks it is the last, as the saying goes. Understand that Ragnarök is *always* coming, and it is something that we cannot hope to understand completely at this stage in our development.

Do not try and get on Loki's good side by slandering the other Gods. You will not impress Loki if you call Freyja a slut or Odin a tranny, you will only reveal your own ignorance. Even insulting His bitter enemies, like Heimdall or Skaði, is a bad idea. Some self-professed Lokeans take inordinate pride in bloviating at great and sapless length about their despite for the rest of the pantheon. The verbosity and unoriginality of their slurs, the thin smear of understanding on which they are based, and the supercilious tone with which these are delivered speak for themselves. You're not bigging up Loki when you call Odin names, you're glorifying yourself for being clever and having picked a better side. (This does not mean that Loki will never manifest anger or resentment towards the rest of the Tivar. He does, and it is terrible to be around. However, Loki is a creature in whom vengeful rage and devotional love can co-exist seamlessly, without contradiction. This is an important part of His nature.)

Sex: This isn't exactly a hazard, as such, but be aware that Loki is a profoundly sexual being. He carries with Him a fair old whack of male sexuality and has a tendency to flirt heavily with people—and more than flirt; if you only ever do one or two workings with Him the question might never come up, but the longer you work with Him the more likely it is. He has a blithe disregard for things like gender identity and orientation, and doesn't care tuppence if you have commitments elsewhere. Generally speaking it's all in good fun, although He can get pretty serious about longer-term relationships. The only people I've known who've worked with Loki for any length of time and not seen this side to Him were people who would have been genuinely wounded or threatened if He'd made advances.

How you choose to deal with the situation is up to you. If you let Him know that you're flattered and all but don't swing that way/have enough partners/don't go around having relations with deities, He'll probably lose interest pretty quickly. You'll have more fun bantering with Him than you will if you turn Him down flat. Don't worry, He enjoys it too.

If you agree to go all the way, He'll either arrange a suitable horse and make love through that person, visit you in dreams or in spirit form, or sort things out on the astral. If you're not sure how one goes about this, Loki would probably be a good person to teach you. I have it on good authority that He knows a great deal about sex magic and may be willing to impart it to the committed student. Be sure to ask what the sex is for. Usually it'll be for fun, but I have heard of it being used to create modifications to the spirit-body—useful, but possibly a bit alarming if one wasn't expecting it.

(NB: This does not mean that Loki or any other being will necessarily be interested in trading sex for spiritual or magical advancement. Some people seem to imagine that the Gods are so desperate to fuck humans that one could learn all Their secrets of in exchange for a few night's entertainment instead of having to study them, rather like a bad porn scenario where a student attempts to get better grades by sleeping with the teacher. The man who brags about how Freyja can't get enough of him and has given up all the mysteries of seidhr, or the woman who claims to have learned everything there is to know about the runes in exchange for a night with Odin is unlikely to demonstrate much knowledge of either.)

Boundaries: Forget it. Loki is all about the transgression of boundaries, yours included. All Gods will challenge you and draw you outside of your comfort zone, leading you step-by-step into new territory. Loki, however, will steam in, rip up all your carefully-erected fences, and burn them. Huge bonfire. Razor-wire melting like candyfloss. Keep Out sign blazing merrily on top of the heap.

Possession: There is some dispute amongst modern heathens as to whether people were possessed by the Tivar in ancient times. Personally, I find the question somewhat redundant, because whatever history relates, the Gods of the North certainly like to engage in possession now. They are Gods Who Like To Party. Odin and Loki in particular are reported to have taken to gatecrashing Vodoun and Umbanda ceremonies if there happens to be someone present who might benefit from talking to them.

Somewhat like the Lwa, it is their nature to ride; unlike the Lwa and other beings who have been regularly invoked over the centuries, They are quite dreadful with boundaries. Loki in particular will think nothing at all of jumping into your head just to raid the fridge. Anything from a light overshadowing to full possession is a possibility, especially if you're one of these people who gets taken over very easily. If you are unhappy with the idea of possession or if it would be unsafe, state this clearly ahead of time and put whatever safety measures you normally have in place. I've included a section on how to handle a Loki possession in the working.

The Working

First off, Loki does not respond well to what's become the mainstream model of working with Gods in a magical context, where the mighty will-full mage hauls divinities down into a magic circle, grabs off a hunk of whatever They've got going, and then sends Them packing with a banishing. Nobody gets conjured, abjured, or otherwise messed with, and nobody's laptop explodes. Treat the exercise as throwing a party at which Himself is the guest of honour. (You should also know that once you've got His attention, He's not necessarily going to wait around for an invite in future. Loki is a bit notorious for dropping in unannounced, sometimes at awkward moments.)

There are a few pre-written Loki-centric rites out there, but I've never been able to get on with them. You probably do not want to go completely free-form, but do not try to use a Wiccan or HCM format and just plug Loki's name into it. I would also suggest avoiding the use of Thorsson's hammer rite in this context, unless you're very attached to it. Instead, I'm going to offer a loose ritual outline which can be adapted to suit your own way of working.

For a brief chat, you can simply take a suitable beverage out to the crossroads one night, drink a toast to Loki and pour out the rest. Hang around to see if He has anything to impart, then go home. A more advanced working is presented below.

The harrow (altar).

I like to include the following:

A red cloth.

A blót-bowl.

A drinking vessel, preferably a horn.

A small branch with lots of twigs, or a bunch of red-coloured flowers.

Spare dishes and bowls for food offerings. These should either be special ritual items that you don't use the rest of the time, or paper plates that can be discarded.

An icon of Loki. Use your favourite picture, or better yet make one yourself. Images of people or characters that put you in mind of Loki are also good—Q from Star Trek is a popular one.

Lots and lots of candles. Some say this is asking for trouble; I say that half the point of the exercise is to ask for trouble. I like to start off with a couple of plain white candles just to clear the air, and then add a big red candle in the centre and lots of tea lights round the outside. Red is the best colour but you could also include bright orange and deep pink. Generally speaking, He seems to prefer heavy florals and spicy fragrances over fruit.

Incense. I use cinnamon and dragon's blood. He also likes chocolate and coffee fragrances and things with silly names.

Ground red pepper, sprinkled on the harrow.

Lay in a good supply of offerings for Loki. Loki's preferred drinks include very strong coffee, orange Tang, high-caffeine energy drinks, cheap beer and, just to be contrary, any decent single-malt Scotch whiskey. Good foods include the kind of thing you might have at a child's birthday party such as little cakes and sweets. I hear He's very partial to Peeps, those marshmallow chicks you can buy in the States around Easter. Cooking Him a meal is usually well received—go for something rich and involving ridiculous amounts of melted cheese. If you eat meat or fish yourself, include some of those (He taught me how to poach tuna steaks in beer, which He seems to enjoy). He sometimes appreciates a bowl of hot soup.

You can also offer Him heart-meats. That tends to bring out His nature-red-in-tooth-and-claw side, but He really appreciates it. Cook the meat down into a stew or burn it up in a fire.

Loki likes tobacco. This should be in the form of the most revoltingly cheap smokes you can get your hands on, or cloves. Dedicate the cigarette to Him and smoke half, breaking open the rest and burning it like loose incense. If you don't smoke, you should still try and take a token puff, or at least breathe a little of the smoke as it burns in the incense bowl.

Miscellaneous: You might want to keep on hand some or all of the following items. It's possible that you won't end up using any of this stuff, but believe me, it can come in very handy at times: Toys and shiny things. Party favours for small children. Things that flash, bang or whiz—if fireworks can be arranged, so much the better. Dress-up clothes, costume jewellery, cosmetics, face paints, body paint etc.

Art supplies. These should not be too fiddly or serious, no ultra-fine Rotrings or expensive oil paints; choose things you won't mind getting used up very quickly. Think big rolls of paper, felt-tips, stickers, fingerpaints, poster colours, thick crayons, glue, glitter, clay, and Plasticine or Fimo.

Props for whatever else you normally do for fun. I'm sure you'll think of something.

A good technique if you're not sure what to offer is to take the God shopping. Go down the shops and ask Him to come with you and poke you if there's anything He'd like. Your trip should include food shops, one of those girly accessory places that sell angel wings and glittery make-up, a confectioners and a toyshop.

The Calling

Having something to recite can really help get your head in the game. There are pre-written evocations you can use, but you should adapt these freely or better still compose your own from scratch. The list of kennings given above makes a good starting-point. Kick off with something like "hail to Loki..." "honour to Loki" or "we call on Loki..." You might want to leave out the parts referring to Geirrod, as this is not a stellar episode in His career, and include more modern kennings for Loki. I call Him "Mother of Witches." Many of us call Him Hot Stuff or similar. You could also try and make up your own. Names referring to fire, handsomeness, love, rage, wit, shapeshifting and magic are good. Do not include gender or sexual slurs unless they could also be applied to you.

Make the piece long enough to get everyone thoroughly involved and revved up, but don't make it tedious and over-written. If Loki thinks you're too in love with the sound of your own voice, it's likely He won't bother to show up and may arrange an uncomfortable object lesson in humility. Likewise, do not write a grovelling piece. Kneeling before Loki will get you exactly two things—a sleazy grin and a "while you're down there..." Big Him up, but be sincere about it. Speak from a place of genuine reverence and love, or don't speak at all.

Getting Down to Business

Clear your ritual space in your preferred manner, then set up the temporary harrow. You might want to light some white candles and burn a little incense. Get everyone into the right kind of headspace with a few beers and some tea or coffee. Ideally you should all spend some time kicking back, laughing, discussing Himself and related topics. If people are feeling anxious or concerned, now would be a good time to air those fears.

If you are working solo, spend some time relaxing, reading Loki-related texts, meditating, reflecting on Loki's mysteries. It's a good idea to take a bath or a shower before changing into your ritual clothes, if worn. These should be comfortable and allow for ease of movement; for preference they should be red or mostly red and pretty to look at. I personally favour a pair of red satin pyjamas.

Go into the ritual space and light all the candles and the incense. If you're using cigarettes, light one; if not use incense or smudge. Blow the smoke around the room and say "I hallow this space in the name of the Gods" or a similar phrase. You might want to make the hammer sign in the air, with your hand, the smoking item, or with a hammer if you have one.

Now recite the calling. If you have drums and noisy items, get banging. (The Tivar don't seem to care much for rattles—they like drums, sometimes with bits of rattly stuff hung off the sides). Get everyone to join in if they like—leave gaps in your recital so that people can repeat the line or jump in with their own contribution. Don't worry about deviating from the text and improvising; equally, don't fret too much about whether the scene is wild enough. Just let it happen.

If it's just you, take full advantage of that fact. Let yourself get carried away. You are not at a middle-school poetry recital. Sway your body, move your hips, chant and dance. Let the words come as they will. Let your voice rise and fall. If the urge comes over you to abandon your prepared text altogether and run round the room screaming and laughing, then that is what you should do.

When you feel either that Loki is present at the rite or you've called enough for one night, take the drinking vessel and fill it with your chosen libation. Take a swig, say "Hail Loki!" or similar and pass it to the next guy. If anyone feels inspired to add a bit more, go for it, but don't hog the limelight.

The Sacrifice

In pre-Christian times, a sacrifice to the Gods would have been a farm animal, or sometimes a person. For a sacrifice to Loki, I recommend getting one of those little clockwork toys that sparks. Have everyone touch it and speak any message they want to offer to Loki. Wind up the toy, let it go on a flame-proof surface and set fire to it. You might need to dunk it in lighter-fuel, but it looks great once it's going. You might also wish to sacrifice some pornography by burning, or the aforementioned marshmallow abominations (this last can also be done in the microwave). Anything that burns, smashes or explodes is good. You might also wish to offer some physical act dedicated to Loki—I generally offer a feat of heat-resistance. Otherwise the sacrifice can be the meal I mentioned earlier, and you can speak your message to Loki as the horn or shared ritual meal goes round. (I suggest you do not petition Loki for anything at this point. Get to know Him a bit first, preferably over a few months.)

Take up the blót-bowl and fill it with liquor. Dedicate it to Loki—trace Gebo, the gift-rune over it, then whichever rune you most associate with Loki—Kenaz is the one that speaks loudest to me of His nature so I use that. Dip the twig in the liquid and splash a little onto the harrow and onto each of the participants. Bless them in the name of Loki.

Leave some of the goodies on the harrow for Loki. A decent portion of the ritual meal, over which you have sketched Gebo and Kenaz. Crack open one of the beers, sketch the runes in the air and pass the can through them. Invite Loki to enjoy the beer through you, and take a good long swig. Leave the rest on the harrow for the God. Do the same with the sweets and other drinks. Be generous. Loki was bound in that cave for an endless time, cold and without food or drink, so when He comes to visit you should feed Him well and make Him welcome. (Don't consume the food or drink once it's been left on the harrow and dedicated. The God should be understood to have had all the 'foodness' out of it—it's no longer good to eat. You should dispose of it respectfully, preferably pouring it out onto the earth, burning or burying it.)

After that... well, what happens, happens. Your first encounter might be pretty intense; my first serious working in this vein involved dancing to hallucinatory music, chain-smoking, losing about four hours and waking up in different clothes and with a fresh brand on my arm. I think He likes to give you a bit of a rough ride the first time round just to see what you're made of. Just stick with it and don't chicken out and do something stupid like performing a banishing. It probably won't work and you might make Him decide you need toughening up.

Dance, sing, or sit quietly as the mood takes you. Listen to Loki, see what He has to say. Pay attention to all of your senses. You may find that parts of your body get very hot, or that you get strange visual, auditory or olfactory sensations. You may get very direct auditory communication, or you may get something more nebulous. I usually receive a brew of sensory information, sounds, colours, textures, ideas, and sometimes an audible voice in the ear. You may be given tasks to perform, information, or advice. Sometimes all Loki wants to do is play—He's a people person and really enjoys being around humans.

Possession

Assuming you find yourself dealing with a Loki possession, how should you approach it? At the time of writing I have never horsed Loki in company, so the following is all third- and fourth-hand. First off, do not allow your visitor to get bored. Keep Him entertained with conversation, singing and dancing, and His preferred offerings—food, drink, toys etc. It is best to designate a specific individual to act as a wrangler, someone to stay with the horse at all times and keep the God entertained. Be aware that Loki is very grabby with His wranglers—one person jokingly referred to the job as being a chew toy—and take that into consideration when you sort out who's doing what. Loki delights in playing fast-and-loose with your boundaries—coming down into a male horse and making a beeline for the straightest guy in the room, for example. The caveats about how to behave around Loki are obviously very important for this situation.

The Closing

Go on until you physically can't handle any more or you feel the presence withdraw, then perform a closing. Thank Loki for being with you—sincerely thank Him, no matter what has transpired. Tell Him the party is over and you'd like to rest now. Understand that He may not withdraw entirely for some days.

(I really mean it about that banishing ritual.)

Ground yourself by whatever means you prefer. Perhaps wash again, change your clothes, and go out for a walk or maybe a bite to eat. You should at least go into another room and do something to clear your head. The participants should give each other support and thanks, and have whatever discussion is necessary to part on a positive note. Bear in mind that everyone might need a little while to process what they've experienced, even if it seemed quite subtle, and the full effects of the working may well take a while to percolate.

Conclusion

I've now been doing indescribable Loki-related stuff for just over a year and a half and, as He enjoys reminding me, I've got a long way to go. Take all of the above with a pinch of salt, your mileage may vary, do not taunt happy fun ball, etc.

It's brutally hard at times, but the rewards far outweigh the difficulties. Loki has given me experiences I could never even have imagined before I encountered Him. He has burned up years of accreted mental garbage and helped me to break out of stultifying patterns of thought and behaviour that have kept me trapped in one corner of my life. Loki has many gifts to offer but His greatest gift to me has been the fire that sweeps away the dead wood and allows the new growth to blossom. Burn it all up. Burn up the doubt. Burn up the fear. Burn up the confusion and the uncertainty and the *whatever will the neighbours think* and the twitch in the brain that kicks and says "you're wrong and the other guy's right." One day all that detritus will be a bonfire, and the bonfire will be ash, and the ash will blow away on a hot gale and there will only be Loki.

Most of all, His fire transforms. Understand that whatever you were before you entered His borne, you will not be the same afterwards.

Good luck.

Loki

Thunorwine

Hail to Loki!
Trickster to gods and men,
bringer of creative chaos,
perserver of the nine worlds.
I offer drink to you;
remembering Woden's oath,
I pour out my sacrifice
into the sacred fire.
We drink together as friends
and will depart as friends from this
and all future blots.
Hail Loki!

Honor to Loki

Silence Maestas

Hail to Loki
lightfoot and sly;
wind walker
swift talker
knave of the Aesir court.
We salute the Mother,
the Father, the God:
Laufey's illustrious son.
Crackling and bright
you catch our kindling
and gladly we burn for you.
Thief of hearts,
Lover, Beloved and Blessed;
passion your playground and
torment your touch;
emotional arson is yours.
Cruelly you cut and
cruelly you kiss;
with glee are worlds made anew.
Honor to Loki, honor to Lopt,
honor to Hoenir's Friend.
Honor to the one who keeps
worlds out of balance;
honor to He who sets right!

Tale of the Anti-Hero
Karen Emanuelson

Who is this Loki: trickster, thief?
He does not always stay to fight,
The glorious, ever celebrated battle.
Brave, true and fearless? No, he runs.

Or flies, shifting into many forms,
Many lives, a man who is sometimes
Female. He is the God of mothers;
a mother, too, of wondrous Sleipnir,

Silver, eight-legged stallion. Loki's foal.
Swiftest of all, of any horse, ever after.
Praise to Loki, God of mischief, chaos
and lies. All stories are lies ... even this.

Patron of Storytellers, Loki sits with Arapaho,
Helping to spin their tales of Coyote, their trickster.
How he is always going along, and even killed,
Coyote goes along. He is the regenerating God.

One story leads into another,
Another story, another life, always.
The stories change, framed in same.
The God is born again, and shifts.

Loki embodies the midnight sun,
Born of fire and ice. His dark hair curls
like smoke from campfires where stories
Are conceived; light fighting off dark.

His eyes shift from green to blue,

From red to yellow, seething lava.
Loki's children include the world serpent
And Fenrir, the wolf who destroys.

Loki is fast, strong and lethal.
He can kill with a word.
A skilled warrior, he exchanges
His axe and sword for his harp.

Lover of many women who are wives
Of others, Loki loves life, loves women.
He has been a woman, too. He knows
The pain, the ebb and flow. The tides.

He is beautiful in face and form,
This dark-haired God with the changeling
eyes. The midnight sun burns, light shines
through, hints of red flash from his hair.

He is the father of Storytellers
And Loki is the mother of tales.
His journeys are adventures ... or not.
Some are songs which are stories.

Lies and truth.

Contemplating A Tour

Karen Emanuelson

Should I go with Loki on some rash quest
Or mis-adventure? Why in Hel's name should
I trust him when the Gods state he's a pest?
He'll get us killed or banished at least, would
That be worth my while? I don't want to have
My lungs torn out of my back: Blood eagle?
If that's the result of our trip, I'll pave
No new ground for myth and keep things legal.
Loki, the shape-shifter, trickster and thief–
Here he comes now to try to plead his case.
His eyes change from gold to blue in his grief.
Why should I always eat blame for my race?
Take my hand, we will become birds and fly
The nine worlds. Come see, then ask me why.

Many of us who love both Odin and Loki have long believed, suspected or known that there was more to the two of Them swearing "blood brotherhood" than initially meets the eye. As deep as the animosity may be between Them, so deeply runs the love, desire and molten hot passion. –GK

Fulltrui

Elizabeth Vongvisith

In the lands of my people
the drumbeat of the blood
sends us to each other—
bound by its scarlet call,
we answer to ourselves, our desires
unshadowed, uncloaked
in silence or shame, regardless
of to whom the blood gravitates us
with its magnetic pull.

So it was in my homeland,
O heart's friend, that I felt you there
circling closer, nearing me inexorably
as the day drew to a close
and mantled the forest in darkness.
The daylight flamed in the west,
closing its doors and letting
night steal in to draw the bed-hangings.

All throughout
the chase that day,
I sensed you watching, your eye
as gray as dawn,
resting like the self-assured touch of a lover
against the back of my neck,
the barest kiss of awareness.

When we brought down the stag,
exultant in our shared triumph,
I could have taken you then,
sweat-covered and speckled in blood,
but I chose to let the hunt continue a little longer
until both predator and prey were subdued.
So instead I held out to you
the steaming liver of our quarry
and watched as your strong teeth
sank into the flesh.

I asked you then,
Would you bind yourself further,
grim-hearted one? and you
did not balk or recoil when I instead
held out my own bleeding arm.
When you had cut yourself and tied
your forearm to mine, I could feel
time shift, the Worlds still for a second
in their ceaseless spinning,
a decision made—
or perhaps it was just the ache in my groin
and the fever I tried not to let you see.

Then Nott
threw the hangings closed
and the sky deepened to black
overhead, the stars so radiant
that I could see your bloodstained smile
before you turned away to go wash
in the stream tumbling from the hillside,
muscles flexing under hide—
and then,

yes,
the hunt was over.

Your ferocious grip startled me
as much as the heat and hunger
from your mouth.
I wondered briefly exactly who
had caught whom, but then,
slowly, deliberately,
the way a maiden unlaces her shift
for the first time,
you took your mouth from mine,
lifted your face to the sky
and bared your throat, knowing exactly
what you were doing.

That beast who lives in me
sensed surrender, snarled and
clamped its jaws on your shoulder
to pin you down, to devour you—
Ymir's murderer, enemy of my ancestors,
writhing in my arms as if longing were
made into a thing of nerves and skin,
my brother, my love,
impaled by my flesh, back arched—
us two mating wildcats,

our hunt concluded in swift and silent acknowledgment
and your spear lodged deep in my spirit.
From that day I was and am forever your fulltrui,
for good or ill, love and love's pain,
despite the stony road before us both
and the blood and fire waiting at its end.

Untitled

Silence Maestas

I'd like to teach my fool tongue to dance
to tap out a rhythm rhymed sure
that sparkles and leaps
singes and licks
at vocabulary's luscious provide.
I'd serve up a banquet of wit and riposte
to challenge a champion's chant
that ripples and wonders
and resonates to win
the poet's acclaimed admiration.
I'd sketch you in sound, use syllables to paint
to color a page with prose
that astounds and reveals
absorbs and resounds
through the long fickle favor of ages.
I'd give voice to your wonder, declare you the most
dearly wicked of endless endearments.
But you torment and gloat
torture and goad
at my tangled tongue's rusty replies.

An Orchestra in Twenty-Six Parts
Silence Maestas

A is for Apple, immortal and gold,
B is for Brother, your partner in crime;
C is for Clever, your wisdom untold,
D is for Deviance, transgression sublime.
E is for Echo, dogging my thoughts,
F is for Fool, both mocking and true;
G is the Game where you toss the lots,
H is for Heart, the one I gave you.
I is Illuminate—you light where I go,
J is for Jest, when life needs a shove;
K is for Kettle, the Grove that I know,
L is for Loki, for luck, and for love.
M is the Magic you brought to my life,
N is for Naglfar, the ship you will steer;
O for Opportunity resulting from strife,
P is the Promise I hope is sincere.
Q is for Question, your riddle profound,
R is for Romance—a weapon, it's true;
S is for Speech, both silence and sound,
T is for Truth, troublesome and new.
U is Uninvited, the way you arrived,
V is the Value that you find in me;
W is the Wreck from which I revived,
X is XXX, three kisses times three.
Y is the Youth I've giv'n to your task,
Z is your Zeal when you rip off my mask.

Twenty-six letters, twenty-six notes
to compose my life and script my desire.
Twenty-six moments, twenty-six motes
to color my experience and my heart inspire.
This is my orchestra in twenty-six parts—

twenty-six new songs you taught me to sing.
Twenty-six reasons to continue to bring
you into my life and into my heart—
for you, dear Loki, I've raised love to an art.

Invocation to Loki
Pagan Book of Hours

Laufey's Son,
Trickster of the far north,
Delicate spawn of giants,
Wheedler and coaxer with the secret agenda,
Liar who speaks the truth others will not hear,
We call you, two-faced one whose soul burns bright,
And invite you to be critical of our souls.
You love to make us break our vows,
When those vows are made heedlessly.
You love to catch us in our own hypocrisies
And puncture our bubbles of pride.
Nothing is safe from you, no emotion
Is sacrosanct from your prodding.
What do we really think, you ask?
What are we not saying? You know,
And your shifty eyes catch ours,
Your crafty smile slips across your face,
And we blush in shame, knowing
That you have read our foolish fumblings
With the truth. For the truth is a flame that burns,
You tell us. Do not pretend to eat fire
If you are not willing to suffer the consequences,
Which is to be cast out by others.
Only when we are clear-eyed and humble
Will your gaze toward us be free of slyness.
Loki, Spirit of Truth and Lies,
Burn us with the measure of our own words.

Loki

Galina Krasskova

Oh my beloved God,
You have feasted upon my heart.
You have devoured it,
as though it were the sweetest of fruits.
My fine and feral God:
savage and sensual all at once;
compassionate and cruel,
my heart was ever too small a thing
to hold the secrets You whispered in the dark
and far too small for Your brother's furious thunder.
I have danced in Your flame.
I have made my bed in its sweetness.
I have felt its bite and its silken caress.
You have ridden the pulsing gallop of my heart beat,
swam the rivers of my blood.
I have poisoned myself with you,
my Intoxication, my Addiction, my God.
Nowhere could I flee, if ever I wished to flee
from the implacable heat of Your presence.
Loki, before even Odin there was You.
And in my heart, some halls remain hidden for You alone.

My Beloved Conundrum

Galina Krasskova

Heat of my heart
Fire that rides the bone-steed of my blood,
If Odin "speaks to me in riddles and speaks to me in rhyme,"*
as the poets say,
then You, my bright-haired, emerald-eyed, teasing God,
are the riddle and rhyme in one.
You, my lean and hungry predator,
are the answer to every question,
the question in every answer,
every secret, every lie,
every truth grudgingly told,
and every sweet-lipped, foreboding murmur.
You are the willowy terror of drowning waters
and the laughing cruelty of the hungry flame.
Salmon and fly, flea and seal, cunning hag and winsome maid
but always Loki, always You Yourself,
in every form, in every shadow,
in every flickering, tremulous moment of being.
And I adore You,
and count Sigyn lucky
to call Your arms Her home.

---

* This particular phrase is part of the song "Possession" from the album of the same name by Sarah McLachlan. Many Odin's women feel that this stanza and the one following it powerfully reflect the hold the Old Man has on them.

Courting the Trickster
Sophie Oberlander

I am always amused by the reactions I get when it becomes known that I am dedicated as gythia to Loki (and Odin too, but the Old Man seldom evokes such a strained response). No other God or Goddess seems to inspire quite the same degree of discomfort, or in some cases outright hostility, as Odin's blood brother. It often saddens me to see how Loki is approached, for invariably the methods fall into one of two categories: either he is spoken of in jesting terms, and His name evoked to allow for expiation of any number of foolish acts, or He is regarded with suspicion, hostility and no small degree of fear. But Loki is far more than the sum of lore, and like any Trickster, resists such neat if derogatory compartmentalization.

The fact that Loki is a trickster is certainly not up for debate. It is His role, nature and function that are often misunderstood. The word 'fool' is often applied to trickster figures such as Loki, though it does not carry quite the same connotation as one might think. In the medieval period, the fool was often the only member of the court who could speak painful truths to the king without facing possible execution. As such, the fool as an archetype is a figure unhindered by societal constraints. He is not a 'safe' or comfortable figure and has a disconcerting tendency to alter all rules and mores to fit His own desires. However, one must explore exactly what the ultimate goal of any Trickster's actions is.

While it is true that Loki (or indeed any God that chooses for Himself the role of Trickster—and it is interesting but most trickster gods are male) can create a state of extreme discomfort and annoyance, I would posit that if He shows up, there is always a reason for His presence. What may on the surface appear to be totally uncontrolled chaos can then be regarded as coldly calculated strategy, with the Trickster as the vehicle of truth.

Loki is the enemy of entropy and complaisance, and He fights it with a vengeance. He is the enemy of a heart without passion, devoid of devotion. He can be wrenchingly cruel to His children, but in hindsight it is never 'cruelty', but rather the firmness of a parent to an erring child. And therein lies the secret to His motivation (as irritating as that may be to those of us who would choose to believe that we are beholden to no one): He forces us into accepting the full weight of our *wyrd*, into opening to the myriad ways in which the Gods may inspire us, to actively claiming our own potential and the responsibility that comes with it. He can be a bastard, it's true (and I say this loving Him dearly) but He's a bastard with a purpose.

I won't say that my relationship with Loki has always been easy, but I will admit that it was through Him, more than any other that I came to define the spiritual journey as a process of falling in love with God. I was very fortunate in the early stages of my growth as gythia. I started out dedicated to Odin and over the years it was He who first led me to Loki. I knew the stories of course but put little stock in lore. There is a great temptation, especially in reconstructionist religions like Asatru, to cling to lore, to hold to it as sacred gospel, using it to define and compartmentalize one's spiritual world. The spiritual journey, however, cannot and will not be safely delineated in such a fashion (yet another lesson from my beloved Trickster) and when lore alone defines that journey our souls wither in their shells. Many people hold to lore staunchly because they are afraid to hold to God, afraid of the implications of Gods that aren't neat cardboard stereotypes or archetypes but living, loving, passionately manifesting beings. Lore is important only when one knows how to interpret it otherwise it is a useless crutch and blockage to the spiritual experience (all the more so when one cannot move beyond its literal interpretation). The Gods cannot be and are not defined by words dead on a page, but reveal Their wisdom to eyes trained in the exploration of the patterns and rhythm of divine being and *wyrd*. Having come to this conclusion early on as a result of my own personal experiences with Odin, I was not bound by any preconceptions regarding His brother's nature and was able to allow my relationship with Loki to develop naturally. And develop it most certainly did!

Loki has caused me more fear and discomfort than any other God that I have ever honored, called or worked with and I thank Him for it. He has forced me to stretch the boundaries of my understanding to the breaking point and beyond gently (and sometimes not so gently) pointing out areas where I fall short, especially in my faith, troth and trust. Then in His own inimitable way, He began to teach me. His presence is a constantly palpable thing in our kindred and for one of our members He smoothed the process of her rather rocky transition from southern Baptist to Heathen. Having observed Loki's actions within our own Kindred, I've come to realize that He acts as a catalyst and facilitator of personal growth. And with that growth may come the inevitable growing pains.

The Trickster is not an easy one to face or to accept, and not only because boundaries are irrelevant to Him. He forces us to examine in minute detail our own shadows, egos and facades. He is the most powerfully kinetic instrument of truth revealing what is meaningless and unhealthy in a way that is utterly pure; odd though it may be to associate purity with Loki. The inherent difficulty in this is the element of sacrifice integral to His nature. Interestingly enough, for all that the Trickster may challenge us in facing our own masks, that very role of 'trickster' is but a mask that He himself dons. What lies beneath that varies: intense grief and pain, compassion, ecstasy ... I would definitely call Loki a God of ecstatic union. In my seidhr-work, I have had experiences of witnessing Loki standing at the foot of the Tree weeping as Odin hung, and certainly I've had hints that there is more to Their relationship than is ever recorded in lore. More than anything else, Loki is a God that demands, at least of his women, utter surrender to passionate union. He can be playful, raunchy, crude, sarcastic (and my Gods He is never silent; I've had running conversations with Him throughout my day and His commentary on mortal nonsense is stimulating to say the least), tender and eliciting a vulnerability that I would have denied I was capable of, fiercely protective, and coldly compelling. But one thing that I have never in ten years of working with Him seen Him be is cruel for cruelty's sake.

Perhaps the key to understanding Loki is striving to see through His eyes for I'm certain that the Gods' perception of our wyrd is quite different and far more encompassing that our own could ever be. I would never hesitate to suggest that a student talk to Loki and that is one of the secrets to truly bonding with one's Gods: simple conversation, just as one would converse with a loved one in person. I've found Him to be one of the easiest Gods to contact, to feel intimately and directly; getting Him to go away is totally different story! One of the greatest gifts that Loki has given me was introducing me to His bride Sigyn, and that has opened up a completely unexpected door in my spirituality. Experiencing the Gods on such a personal and direct level certainly takes nothing away from Their Divine nature; rather it enhances our own connection and understanding of it.

One area in which Loki's influence on me has been profound is my role as teacher and spiritual counselor within my kindred. I had a Wiccan once, after seeing me in action, speculate that my totem animal must be a pit-bull! As Loki does not move within a person's comfort zone, so through Him have I as gythia been taught to rip away a student's comfort zone so that they may approach their people, Gods and life from a position of truth and clarity not based on egotism, fear or conformity. This can often be harsh but the results are definite and undeniable. Of course, I also have a tendency to make extremely off-color and/or rude comments at unexpected times, which is a less complimentary offshoot of being devoted to Him. Basically, Loki stirs things up, having little interest in maintaining the spiritual status quo. There is a line in "Dreams of Isis" by Normandi Ellis: "Despite our best efforts to remain the same, we shall all be changed." And that is Loki in action.

Trickster

Sophie Oberlander

I never sought You.
Those places deep within my heart were far too burned and scarred
to let You in, hard like misshapen stone.
Or so I thought.
But I gave much
the first time I hung on that Tree.
Not enough, by far, but just enough to shatter that wall of stone
the barest fragment breaking free.
I heard Your whisper, but turned aside my face...
You could not be speaking to me.
I felt Your gentle touch cradling my wounded spirit
as You cradled Odin,
His body bloodied, His spirit on fire beneath that Tree
long before I climbed its branches.
Was it through Your laughter that You taught me to love You?
Or through the tenderness of Your caress?
I have seen a face of You that few bother to see.
I have felt Your burning passion, gentle and tender
beneath the Tree.
Brother, Lover, Friend,
No image of God quite prepared me for You.
You eased away my terror with Your wicked cavorting,
making a broken child laugh by playing the fool.
I have seen Sigyn's quiet contentment,
and the love behind Your games.
I no longer understand the trepidation
in which others call Your name.
I have seen Your other face too,
when You took me to Your daughter's realm.
I have seen You, locked in ecstasy
summoning up Her wards and wights for me.

My heart's stone did not so much break
as melt beneath Your flame.
I have tasted Your rage, Your fury at my hurt,
reveled in the darkest glee
with which You opened the gates of Niflheim to defend me.
No one told me how much You cherish Your children.
I have seen You, Trickster, weeping in anguish
every one of Your childrens' wounds piercing Your heart.
And I have seen You in battle, Odin's equal,
though Yours a far darker art.
I have heard Your song, far sweeter than I ever knew it could be,
as You took my hand, and led me from that Tree.
If it Your stories I cherish most, as we walk Bifrost bridge,
dancing patterns amongst the stars.
You placed my hands upon the web, and taught me songs to weave.
As I hung for Asgard, through You, for Hela's realm I reached.
I know how You are feared, or mocked, or thought long bound.
But I know too, it was Your hand
guiding me through my darkest despair and pain.
And how can I fear Your deepest love,
when it is the freedom of my heart I've gained?
Loki, now it is Your burning that I seek.
Let us mingle songs beneath the Tree,
for I adore the flame You have ignited in me.

For Loki
Granuaile

I frequently deliver apples for Idunna, it is how I have come to know the Nine Worlds and meet many of the Gods and Wights. On one occasion, I delivered apples to Loki and Sigyn in the cave where Loki is (sometimes) "imprisoned". This was a new aspect of Loki to me; prior to this delivery I had always experienced Loki as unbound. I could not help staring at Loki chained to a rock. It made me think of the image of Prometheus. Loki noticed me staring. "I want to thank you for the delivery of apples—Sigyn so needs them—but before you go, grant me a boon," he said. "The next time Sigyn empties the bowl, bow your head between my body and Skadi's serpent and feel the poison drip on your skin. Spare me the pain of one drop and feel the Trick it works. Do this for me as a sign of frith and I will be your teacher and ally." As Sigyn moved to empty her bowl I bent over, bowing my head over Loki's body and felt a drop of the poison fall on my skin.

As the drop fell on the back of my neck and trickled down my spine, the poison tore through me. It sucked all the heat from my body like a freezing winter wind. It made my skin burn and ache to my core like the deep, bitter cold that can settle into your exposed skin and frozen limbs on cold, windy, winter night, but it also quickened my heart rate and my senses like speed, fear, and adrenaline. I knew this rush could become addictive to a mortal like me.

Images and thoughts sped through my mind and my vision with painful clarity. I felt as though the poison was somehow meant to check the force of dynamism in the Worlds, but not to arrest it; to somehow focus the virile power of Loki without subjugating him entirely. The poison was like a good cold, snowy, winter is for a garden. By the freezing of the body and the quickening of the spirit, it is just enough to *winter-over* the seeds so they can germinate and flourish in the spring. I felt somehow that this punishment and torture fuels Loki's irrepressible strength and energy, triggering it in massive bursts that split consensual reality, causing our subjective worlds to quake.

"Thanks," I said.

"See you around," Loki said with a wry smile and a wink.

I had this vision about a year ago and I've thought a great deal about this experience. I am still processing it. I am still not sure what it all means, not sure of my interpretations of what I felt and saw. Every time I go back to that vision to explore it further it takes on new or different nuances of meaning. Tricky, ha!

Thanks, Loki, for the lessons that freeze me in shocked wonder about what I just experienced and then grow so vigorously into new ways of viewing the world and my place in it. I pour for You.

Drop Dead Loki

Sigrun Freyskona

"stop making me weird"

When I was a little kid, I was "different", to put it politely.

I began reading and writing at the age of two, and used to amuse myself for hours on end with the Oxford English Dictionary on my lap, trying out new words. I was never much for socializing with other children, and the only TV I was allowed to watch was Sesame Street (which I still love to this day) and Mister Rogers' Neighborhood, and occasionally MTV because I could sing along with the songs in perfect pitch (this is when MTV actually had music videos), and later, taught myself to play them by ear on the piano.

I had a rather close relationship with my father's German-born grandfather. Half the time I didn't understand him, because he spoke in a mixture of heavily accented broken English, and German, but I understood the message behind his words, and he was fond of giving me piggyback rides and nose kisses. One night when I was three I dreamed he and I were in a green field, and he lifted me up and said, in German, that he was with his God, and with his family. The next day my mom told me Opa died, and I said, "Oh, I know."

Not too long afterwards, I started having recurring dreams of a one-eyed old man wearing a floppy hat and a windblown cloak, carrying a large wooden staff. He never said anything, just watched me, but His face seemed to be soft, and sometimes He would pat my head. Around the same time, I started seeing shiny little people in the flowers, plants, and trees. Then one day I was playing with my Bert doll, and I saw Him. He was tall, and thin, with flaming red hair, similar in color to my mom's and my brother's, but brighter. He was smiling, and I liked His smile.

He came around frequently, much to the dismay of my mother, who was trying to get me to be more "normal". He would tickle me, and say silly things, and I would watch Him change shape into different people and animals and objects (the best analogy I have for this is the character of Odo on *Star Trek: Deep Space Nine*). We would dance together, and He was fond of my singing. He seemed to be the only "person" who really liked me for me, and took an interest in me. My father was often drunk, and sometimes physically abusive to me or my mother. My mother had very bad mood swings, and yelled at me a lot. My brother was only my half-brother and only came on the weekends, and was usually absorbed in his video games or comic books.

My friendship with Him came to a head when I was in Catholic school for first grade. He would suggest that I say things that would make me laugh, but make others upset. I remember as clear as day asking my first grade teacher, Sister Ursula, "Why do you have a beard?" My mom was not Catholic, but was nominally Christian, and I had a picture of Jesus on my wall. I would come home from school and my mom would ask what I learned today. When I told her, she would say, "Oh, that's not true," and teach me contradictory things, and then I would repeat her teachings in school the next day. Between that and my "rude remarks", I was on "the thinking bench", every day, to think about my sins and repent, except I usually thought everything was hilariously funny. After five months in Catholic school, I was expelled, and spent the remainder of the school year with a very nasty old biddy who slammed her yardstick down on my desk and made me wet my pants.

My solace was spending time with Him, talking and teasing and singing and dancing. In the summer between first and second grade, my mom decided to have me put into special-ed for my insistence that the little shiny flower people were real, and my imaginary friend was real.

Special-ed was absolutely horrible. I didn't belong there, and worse, was marginalized by the "normal kids" for being in "the retard class". My special-ed teacher actually told my mother that I would be permanently institutionalized upon adolescence because of my "hallucinations". I was mainstreamed in the middle of third grade because the other kids in my class were either mentally disabled or severely autistic, and they needed more attention than I did. So I was put into a regular classroom, except that the other kids knew I had been in special-ed, and I was branded an outcast for the rest of my school career.

Things were getting worse at home. My dad was getting more violent, and my mom was crying a lot. When my dad spooked me with his screaming or breaking stuff or hitting one of us, my Friend would find me and give me a big hug. He promised that He would get me out of there. In fourth grade, I was talking to my Friend at recess, and a group of kids threw rocks at me and chased me around the playground, calling me names. That night at home, I told my Friend to go away, He was making me "weird". He looked very sad, and He hung around me for a couple of days, but every time I saw Him, I told Him to go away, and finally He disappeared.

In the summer between fourth and fifth grade, my father put a loaded gun to my mother's head in front of me and I berserked for the first time. Full of wild, animalistic rage that even scared me, I ran into my father, headbutted him in the chest, and he dropped the gun. My mother and I left with just a suitcase of belongings, and they were divorced a year later.

When I was fifteen, I was in a very bad place mentally. I was having a hard time at home, dealing with my mother and her abusive boyfriends. I had no real-life friends I could think of. I cried out to God, if He was there, to help me. The next day I was at Waldenbooks and a Scott Cunningham book literally fell on my head. I took this as a sign, and spent the next year as an eclectic Wiccan.

Then I had the dreams again of the Old Man, who I now knew to be Odin thanks to my study of mythology. I had not heard the word "Asatru", so I practiced in a Norse Wiccan context until I was nineteen, read the word "Asatru" for the first time, and began to learn about Heathenry. In the year 2000 I dedicated myself formally as an Asatruar, and the first Asatruar to latch onto me were Folkish types, mainly because they knew I was dissatisfied with Wicca. It's not that Wicca automatically equals "bad", but I wanted something more historically accurate, and I was quite tired of the poor scholarship of Wiccan books out there.

I was not ever very good at being Folkish, for a variety of reasons. It seems after I became Asatru, the Gods took more of an interest in me, and spoke to me very loudly pertaining to "work" to be done. I was diagnosed with bipolar disorder in 2002, but I now believe this was shaman sickness, because my patron God, Frey, initiated a series of events in 2006 that got me off of psych meds, and since I've been med-free I have not had the meltdown which everyone was expecting.

I had joined the Irminen-Gesellschaft, but it soon was made quite clear Irminism was not the path for me. I started having dreams about my red-haired invisible friend, who said, "Guess who I am?" and the problems within the Heathen community grew to epic proportions. By early 2007, I recognized that Loki was bothering me pretty hardcore, so I resigned from the I-G, as I felt my honoring Loki was not accurately representing the organization. I had several Lokean friends, and discovered the Faeroese text "Loka Tattur", as well as the Anglo-Saxon word Saetere (meaning "robber", and a name for Loki), which many believe is the origin for the word Saturday. I hailed Loki in Blot for the first time in March 2007, and have not looked back since.

Loki is a controversial figure in Heathenry, but I get from Him what I cannot get from any other God, and that is drastic necessary change. I also have a close relationship with His wife, Sigyn. The most common argument against Loki is "He's the slayer of Baldur and Odin grieves." It may be that Odin grieves, and we all grieve for the loss of the bright beautiful God, however, I think Loki knew the only way Baldur could survive Ragnarok is if He was in Helheim, besides which, He may have wanted to cheer up His daughter Hela, exiled to that realm in childhood. I think ultimately Loki was doing His (beloved) blood-brother a favor, ensuring the survival of the Aesir and peace for all people after the Ragnarok (which according to my UPG, no one really wants, but may well happen anyway).

If Loki hadn't shown up in my life, I wouldn't have had the childhood experiences that make me more tolerant and understanding of "different" people now, and I wouldn't be in my current Heathen paradigm. I would be another Folkish "more Heathen than thou" Asapope-in-training. Loki has indeed taught me a lot of things about myself, and what the Gods want from me. I choose to remain in the Asatru community so I can be a voice for the "bad Heathens" and perhaps help move Heathenry forward to a place of closer connection to the Gods, more frith among Their Folk, and less political crap.

Hail Loki, one of the few Beings in any of the Nine Worlds to show me kindness and love.

Full Cycle
Michaela Macha

The cave is dark, as the one where he bested Andvari.
The gold he got freed the Aesir from bonds.
Now he lies fettered himself.
He remembers

Pranks and jests
—dangerous, granted—
Showing them life
without masquerade of youth,
or jewels, or hair.
Drip.

They took his gifts
but they never learned
his secrets of change
and looking at unpleasant truths.
Drip. The bowl fills.

How they put everything
they could not deal with
out of sight, or life:
Ymir. The giants. His Ironwood-get.
Drip.

They could not face death.
Even some humans did better.
The bowl fills to the brim,
surface taut as a bowstring-
Drip.
Poison flows
Balder's blood

rushing
tears of nine worlds
gushing
the stream where they caught him
Snake spit burns
like Asgard's curses,
not this!

Tormented, he strains
to break bonds
with prophecy's force
Midgard trembles
—*maybe this time?*—
Sigyn hurries
Will she return...?
Relief.
Now it's just the cave, and the darkness,
and three stones cutting his back,
and the memories they share.

Drip.
A tear Sigyn sheds.

Sigyn: Loki's Gentle Bride

Galina Krasskova

I had been a priest of Odin and friend to Loki for many years, before I ever encountered Sigyn. Up until that point, I had never had a particularly strong or close relationship with any of the Norse Goddesses, so it was a delightful surprise to find myself being strongly drawn to Sigyn, the wife of Loki—all the more so since She is unlike any other Goddess I have ever loved.

There's almost nothing about Sigyn in the lore. She's mentioned three times, in every instance referenced as the wife of Loki who remains with Him when He is bound, dutifully holding a bowl to capture the poison of the serpent, which Skadhi hung above Loki as added torture. It is also noted that She has two sons by Loki: Narvi and Vali, the former of which is killed when Loki is bound. Sadly, she often stands in the shadows of the more popular Asynjur like Freya or Frigga. I have seen Her dismissed as everything from a dutiful doormat to the epitome of the abused wife. Very, very rarely, however, have I ever encountered anyone who has had any type of interaction with this Goddess and I can well understand why: Loki is very protective of His bride. I myself have refused to hail Her in symbel halls where Loki is unwelcome. She, more than any other Deity I have ever encountered evokes a protectiveness in those who know Her that one does not often associate with a God. Of all the things that I have been privileged to learn in my spiritual life, this I know with utter surety: Loki loves Sigyn as He loves no other and She alone holds the key to His heart.

Needless to say, I never expected to fall in love with such an amazingly gentle Goddess. Sigyn initially chose to come to me as a gentle, shy child bride. I had never dreamed that a Deity would choose the appearance of a young person! It was completely beyond my experience, but I have always believed in allowing the Gods to define the nature of Their interactions with us, and so I welcomed Her. How could I not? She was, if it is not hubris to say so, utterly adorable! I was completely charmed by Her innocence, Her playfulness, Her gentle nature. I, who prided myself on being the implacable warrior, was well and truly brought to my devotional knees. Over the next few months, as I began developing a relationship with this Goddess, I found myself often frustrated by the lack of concrete information on Her for I'm sure the manner in which She has chosen to reveal Herself to me may not be how She comes to every single person. Not only was there little to nothing in lore, but no one in the Heathen community that I had ever met or corresponded with honored Her. Thankfully, this has since changed and I've discovered a small number of Sigyn's folk out there but at the time, I felt as though I was the only one. Questions about Her background remain, however. For instance, I'd love to know who Her parents are, whether She's Vanir or Aesir or elf, for instance. I've often had the UPG that She was a foundling, fostered with Njord and His family; a small, waiflike thing that captured Loki's heart the moment He saw Her. A close friend devoted to both Sigyn and Loki believes, conversely, that She must be Jotun, for had Loki married outside of His own race, surely even the Eddas would have noted it. She has a beautiful name for this Goddess she adores: Lady of the Staying Power, for She experiences Sigyn not as a child but as a grown woman, a source of immense security and strength for Loki.

Sigyn comes to me as such a gentle, shy, almost childlike Goddess. The lessons that She brings have been no less transformative then say, Loki's or Odin's but She is gentle and playful about it. Personally, I see Her as a Goddess of love and devotion. She has taught me so much about my own heart, how to see the beauty and divinity in the smallest thing, and how to play ... not something that I ever really did before. Most importantly, She has taught me the value of loving without fear and the strength in gentleness. Anger has been my besetting challenge for most of my life and after passing through years and years of less than subtle lessoning from the various warrior Goddesses, I've found to my surprise that Sigyn has brought an understanding ... that hopefully will lead to mastery and balance. I no longer see showing gentleness as a weakness or my own childlike wonder, which since I was a child myself, I have long hidden away, as a thing to scorn. There is a strength in Her and, when She shows Herself as Loki's wife, in the cave, a grief that often moves me to tears. Yet at the same time, She possesses an elfin inquisitiveness, unguarded sweetness and deep compassion that has allowed Her to open my heart as no other could. Perhaps because She comes in such an unassuming manner, She has the capacity to wheedle into places long barred even to the touch of the Gods. She soothes and I have found Her a willing haven for this particular member of those God-bothered, when the call of duty becomes particularly painful.

She is so sweet, I just cannot come up with another term! There is simply no pretense about Her. When Loki first introduced me to Her, one of the first things I did to honor Sigyn was to set up an altar to Her, just for Her. Needless to say, it turned out to be completely unlike any other altar that I have: there are pretty things on it, stones like rose quartz that I never work with, toys ... She has me buying Her dolls and stuffed animals!! I hate to fall into psychobabble, but I think Sigyn is a Goddess that will help us to heal our "inner child". It's difficult to fight the impulse to nurture Her. Not only do I buy Her toys, what's more, other people with whom I worship have taken to bringing gifts for Her altar, which I find incredibly moving. Sigyn has collected a nice little basket of toys and goodies all Her own. I've come to truly believe that She is the Goddess of the inner child and will heal heart-wounds within us if given half a chance. In Her child persona, She is whimsical and tends to "inflict" that attitude on those who love Her! I don't claim in any way to know how She comes to others, but for me, this is the form She has taken, though once I did see an incredibly fierce aspect of Her, when a child was in danger and She was easily as fierce as Kali Ma, though there was an intense sadness and grief throughout the entire experience.

I suppose I also see Her as a Goddess of neglected children. The best way that I know how to put it is this: Sigyn gathers broken things to Her breast. I've also sensed is a strong connection with Idunna who is a Goddess of immortality, healing, herb lore. Sigyn's magics are, unsurprisingly, gentle: the lore of plants and quiet healing. Her laughter is delightful and She is utterly devoted to Loki. She always seems so very vulnerable to me, a little girl who likes Her toys, likes to laugh, wants to be loved and Loki does love Her dearly. Through UPG, I've come to believe that He must have known Her for years before Their courtship began and I wonder about those years, stories left out of the lore of a time when the Gods were vulnerable and waiting in love.

I must admit, it moves my heart how tender and protective Loki is with His young bride. I knew Him for over two years before He chose to introduce me to Her. And she is so shy, so unbelievably shy. I find myself feeling very, very protective of Her, as if She were a little girl placed into my care. So not only has meeting Sigyn introduced me to another Goddess, one that is healing my heart in ways I never imagined possible; but I have seen quite a different aspect of Loki from what is commonly expected: a loving, tender consort/protector. Sigyn has taught me to open myself and embrace the Gods with the innocence and acceptance of a child. She too strips away the facades and walls and blockages within, but She does it so gently, so very gently that it is a sweet embrace. It seems to me as though even the other Gods relax and become more unguarded when in Her presence and this has granted me yet another immense gift, that of seeing another side to those Gods, like Odin and Loki, that I love. Her words on the matter: even the Gods need comfort sometimes.

Insofar as my offerings to Her go, I find that Sigyn, like many a child, likes fluffy, pretty things, things that inspire happiness and laughter. Flowers are always abundant on Her altar, especially pink roses. Hearts, in the case of my altar, fluorite, labradorite and rose quartz abound. She loves pearls and jewelry of all sorts, and stuffed animals ... especially rabbits, dragonflies and cows (an Audhumla thing, I think. There's a connection with Sigyn and primal creation that I've not been permitted to explore yet). For me, Her sacred herb is milk thistle, though I find pretty much any healing herb appropriate. She also has me collecting keys, a symbol of a woman's authority in the home among the ancient Norse cultures. In fact, She insists that I wear a large, Victorian iron key at my waist at all tribal functions. I occasionally buy Her necklaces, beads: I see Her playing with beads, small, pretty boxes and the like.

There is no worse experience in the world for me than to know that Sigyn is upset. I know also that She is more than capable of coming to a person as a strong, independent Goddess in Her own right. It is simply that for me, this is what She has chosen. I've known other Sigyn's folk for whom it has been much the same. By honoring Her in this fashion, accepting Her choice of guises, I do not intend in any way to disrespect a Goddess whose name after all means, "lady of victory."

Sigyn is one of the most bright-hearted Goddesses I have ever worked with, and She teaches that to Her devotees. Her primary attributes are loyalty, devotion, love, happiness and an almost awe-inspiring innocence. She is, above all else, a Goddess Who opens the heart.

Prayer to Sigyn[*]

Galina Krasskova

Gentle Goddess,
teach me to play.
I've seen the joy You take
in the smallest thing of beauty.
Teach me gentleness,
the sweetness of Your song.
I want to sing, as You sing
when You know Loki is listening.
I wish to be among those nurtured
by Your tender hands,
a bright flower
pruned by Your gentle fingers.
Teach me to love,
as You love:
without condition.

---

* *Previously appeared in* Exploring the Northern Tradition © *2005 Galina Krasskova.*

Sigyn Blessing Oil

Jason Freysson

(For Sigyn in the aspect of a child just coming of age.)

This recipe makes ½ oz. of oil.

Sandalwood oil – 80 drops
Iris (Florentine) oil – 50 drops (this is orris)
Rose Geranium oil – 40 drops
Yarrow oil – 25 drops
Neroli oil – 40 drops
Narcissus oil – 40 drops
25 drops tuberose oil to enhance the narcissus.

Mix into a base of pure sweet almond oil and let sit for at least six days so the individual fragrances can properly blend together.

Sigyn's Song

Given to Galina Krasskova

Scorned they call me.
They tried to keep me away.
My heart lies bound
Tortured for the truth he spoke.
We knew, we knew long ago what would be.
At his birth, I knew they would take my son from me.
I was a child myself, to be given such a choice.
Yet I gave willingly.
My memories, my pain, my rage gathered in the alabaster jar I cherish.
They tried to keep me away—final sacrilege,
As if I would ever deny my heart—
To drag me from his side
When the serpent holding all the fury of Midgard was tied.
They tried.
But how could I leave?
I looked into his eyes.
I looked as he was bound by their fear,
By their shame,
By their bitter, bitter pain.
I saw the grief. I saw the disappointment
That it had come to this,
And I saw the love.
They never did believe how much he loved,
And in loving chose to do what no other would do.
All he ever did came from love,
And a truth, a law so steel-bright-strong
It could never be ignored.
Even we serve the law of the Tree.

I looked into his wounded eyes.
And as my son's flesh was wrapped about his,

I saw his anguish.
How could I leave?
For the first time, I defied them.
I picked up the mask that my husband
Had so willingly worn,
I held it before me in my heart,
And showed them the mirror of blade sharp truth it hid.
For the first time I screamed.
I shrieked through the Tree.
Oathbreakers, all, what he spoke was the truth.
What he spoke was the poison
Reflected back to its source.
For the first time I shrieked, and bloodied
By what was left of my son,
I gathered, becoming stone, the shreds of my pain.
I sat by his side daring them to tear me away.
They could if they wish forget,
They could if they wish desecrate.
But not me.

I stroked his straining cheek,
Lips bleeding though silent was he.
I twined my hand in his. And I captured his pain.
Not a cry did he utter. Not a tear did he shed,
His eyes locked on mine.

And we, each soul torn apart through Ragnarok,
We live, we feel, we bleed.
The poison searing my hands as I shield my heart's face
Is nothing compared to the grief that we see.
They never saw what gift we bore.
They locked us both away
For our treasures are shared between us.
How can there be hope to give

when they have tossed it carelessly into a pit of venom?
I will stay by his side.
He would not leave me in my pain.
I will be healer to all, Mother of all,
For I will be the only one left
To heal the gods from their games.

Victory*

Elizabeth Vongvisith

Not for you the warrior's arms
or the high seat swirled about with smoke
or the jewels of a queen, with the eyes
of a court drawn to you like bees.
Not for you, the glorious ringing call
or even the ghost of a memory among men
except for the fate that awaited you
there on the stony path sprinkled
with your eldest son's drying blood.

They petted you and indulged you
but held you of little account,
Sigyn, despite your name,
and later they said you were only his
because you were too naïve to know otherwise.
So their faithful say still,
seldom naming you among the Aesir.
But I know better than that.

Yours was the firm hand that quieted
the beast inside your love, and yet
rocked the cradles and tended the pots;
the touch of a mother and a lover
ever faithful, ever content inside the walls
of your home and before your hearth
which belonged to him, too.

Yours were the eyes that saw deeper,
past extravagance and pride, past
the jesting and the pained self-assurance

---

* *Previously appeared in* Trickster, My Beloved © *2007 Elizabeth Vongvisith.*

into the churning longing that beat
a rhythm of a desperate, secret desire
to be loved and acknowledged.
You were the first to see that truth.

Yours was the love that gave all, without
expectation or condition, that love
which others only pitied and dismissed.
You were the anchor around which
his furious storm revolved and grew calm.
When another was his roaring match in ferocity,
you were his necessary complement.

And yet they underestimated you
and your loyalty so wordless,
so deep, that when they asked you,
tenacious, gentle one, forced you
to prove it once and for all, they were shaken
by the strength of your devotion.
They underestimated you,
and not for the last time.

When your footsteps took you
underground, when your hands bore before you
the only means you had to succor your love—
when they understood that they had, indeed,
not seen the shadow of strength behind
your careful, gentle smiles,
perhaps then they were regretful.
But you did not care anymore.

For yours was the courage lasting for centuries
despite suffering and doubling your pain
with the pain of the one you love,

despite grief and anger. Yours was the heart
so true and brave that on that terrible day,
as the last of the light vanished
in the clear, sharp violet of your eyes,
all who watched knew then
that the real victory was yours,
no matter what anyone said,
O my Lady of Endurance.

Sigyn's Courage*
Gudrun

Sigyn came to me during a dark time in my life, and brought comfort and strength, more than I could have expected. My first child was born prematurely, and was terribly ill. Even when I could bring her home from the hospital, she still needed a great deal of extra care, and she cried constantly and was always miserable. The pregnancy had been difficult for me as well, with a great many medical problems, and I was weak, ill, hypoglycemic from too much nursing, suffering from a terrible case of post-partum depression to the point of near-psychosis, and then forced through months of sleep-deprivation while caring for my child. My husband of the time commuted hours to his job, and was almost never home, and I was estranged from my blood family over their poor treatment of me, so I was all alone with my predicament. We had very little money, and no sitter in their right mind would have stayed with my sick infant anyway.

Night after night, I walked the floor with my sleepless, screaming child. Day after day, I fed her at my breast, only to watch her vomit up much of my milk from her underdeveloped gastro-intestinal tract that had been rushed too soon into digesting food. She could not digest formula at all, of any kind, so I was her only nourishment. Keeping her fed was a struggle. Keeping her happy seemed impossible. Some nights, when I could finally rock her, half-singing and half-weeping, into a state of restless sleep for a few hours, I would lie on the floor of her nursery, too exhausted to stagger into the bedroom and collapse, waiting with one ear open even in my sleep for her to begin crying again.

One night, I dreamed that I went into a house in the dark. It was a cheap prefab house, dusty and dirty as if no one had cleaned it in a long time, and I remember seeing empty cupboards open with no food in them. I placed my hands on my breasts, which were normally

---

* *Previously appeared in* The Jotunbok: Working With The Giants Of The Northern Tradition *by* Raven Kaldera.

overflowing with milk, as the immense amount of often-wasted milk that I needed to produce to feed her was at least forthcoming as long as I ate constantly, desperately, often with her attached to my teat sucking out the nutrients as fast as I could put them in. In my dream, my breasts were flat and empty, and although I tried to tell myself that this was a dream, I had trouble believing it. I feared that when I woke up, there would be no more milk for my daughter, and she would die, even after all that I had fought to keep her alive.

In the middle of the dusty kitchen, sitting on the floor, was a thin, worn woman in an old shift. Her hair was dry and tangled, hanging to her shoulders, and her face was lined with despair, her eyes glazed over. She rocked back and forth, murmuring to herself. I knelt on the floor next to her and reached out to her, slowly. She looked up, suddenly, and seized my hands. Her eyes met mine, locked onto me, took me with her.

For that moment I was transported into a hideous place. Screams echoed off the stone walls of the underground cavern, screams so harrowing that I wanted to cover my ears. The sight of a rough wooden bowl, burnt in the middle and worn away at the edges, filled with a clear liquid that smoked, gave off fumes that stung my eyes. Sharp stones under my feet as I stumbled to the far side of the cave, blurred vision from fumes and tears, throwing the contents of the bowl against the wall with the eaten-away stone. Then a stumble to the other side of the dark space—must not lose that bowl!—to rinse it in the trickling water, fill it with the brackish stream, then back to the bound figure, to rinse off the poison, dodge the bites of the swinging snake, soothe and comfort and heal the wounds with my tears. Again and again and again, without ending. I would have called it hellish, that place, except that I know that Hel had nothing to do with this place of torment.

I wept with her. I spilled out my pain to her, wordlessly, through choking sobs. I was empty, except for that pain. *How could this happen to me? I did everything that I was supposed to do. I was a good wife. I got pregnant, like I was told that I ought to. All I wanted was the happy mother-child experience, like they write about in all the earthy-crunchy magazines—the mother in the long peasant skirt, smiling, nursing her babe and feeling right with the world, healthy and fulfilled and becoming one with the essence of the Earth Mother. All I wanted was that peaceful home and family, and here I am in a place of torment, through no fault of my own! I have no family now, no kin to aid me. I do not deserve this! I have done nothing wrong!*

I understand, she said to me. *I understand. I understand.* She rocked me, and I rocked her; we rocked together on that hard, dirty floor. *There will be enough*, she said. *You can see it through, and believe that there will be an ending. I believe. I believe that I am strong enough to come to that end.*

"But you did this for love," I whispered, my voice hollow and echoing in the too-silent room. "I don't know if I love her. All I feel is empty. I look at my child and I feel empty. I don't know if I can do this without love."

"There is not only love in this," she said. "There is also Right Doing. The Gods may create a place of torment for you, out of spite or merely indifference, but there is comfort in the Right Doing. Once you have started, you must go on, for who would you be if you abandoned it, after having begun?"

"I don't know if I can take it," I said in a low voice. My arms crossed over my empty breasts. "I don't know how much more I can give."

She reached out both her hands, gently, and placed them on my breasts, and said, "There will be enough to see it through." And, suddenly, there was that rush of pain and the letting-down, and I was full of milk again. I started half-awake; my daughter was crying again and the sound had triggered my breasts to let down and I staggered out of bed, back to my daily grind. As I took my screaming, writhing child from her cradle, I heard the last echo of Sigyn's voice in my mind. "My name means victory," she said.

"Victory," I whispered, as I stuffed the nipple in my child's mouth and held her, hard. The screams were stopped, for the moment. "Victory."

Ah, Sigyn
Ayla Wolffe

Kneeling by the side of your love,
Holding forth the wooden bowl
That catches bitter poison—
Drip, drip, dripping upon his face,
You look with compassion and with pain
Upon the work that has been wrought
By the vengeful hand...
Your son the bonds that hold your love,
Tears stream down your face,
Pure the water that splashes
Upon scourged skin—
A forced smile looks back at you
A fist opens up as if to caress
And love is exchanged.
Your voice resonates,
Singing songs of love and comfort.

When the deed was wrought
The offer that they made,
For you to accompany them,
Back to the citadel,
Back to safety and forgetfulness was made.
You looked on them in rebellion
Dug in your heels.
Stared down the ones who slew your son,
Bound your mate and stayed—
Knowing the loneliness,
The abandon that waited.
Being cast out was your fate,
You carved your *orlog*,
Turned your back and knelt down.

Who could go with the betrayers?
Who could go with those who would ask you
To turn your back on love and comfort?
To leave the memory of touches exchanged,
Nursing a child who had grown to manhood,
Had become exemplary in all ways
Only to be cut down there at your feet.
No, traitor to your heart you could not be.

Living on the edge no stranger to you,
As you lived with your husband
In a place that bordered but never had been
Quite on the inside in any way...
Laughter, love, light
And the smell of something indistinct
That said comforts, safety, home—
That fox red hair,
The rabbit in the pot you cooked,
The little offerings from the forest.
All these spoke of love.

And now you kneel holding a wooden bowl,
Telling the stories of times gone by,
Trying to hold your arms straight,
To keep from shaking, or spilling a drop.
Giving comfort where it can be—
To stroke the writhing etin in his pain.
Ah, Sigyn—such loyalty is but to be rewarded.
And yet no one speaks your name,
No one looks upon your countenance
Or gives you credence
Or sympathy—
Ah Sigyn—
I Hail Thee.

Visiting Sigyn
Granuaile

In August 2007, Sigyn's son Narvi asked a shaman in the presence of a Sigyn's woman to bring one of Idunna's apples to His mother in the cave. This woman asked several folk until she found a person, Granuaile, who could make such a delivery. This is Granuaile's account of that journey. Interestingly enough from the perspective of Divine confluence, years ago I asked Sigyn what rune was best associated with Her and She named nauthiz: need or constraint. –GK

I have had a deep connection with Idunna which goes back to my early childhood with my grandparents. Idunna uses me quite a bit to make deliveries for Her, and it is by this function that I have become acquainted with the Nine Worlds and those who live there. I was glad to be able to make this envoy, because I really enjoy being able to be useful to Idunna, to Whom I owe so much, but also because it gives me a reason to visit with Loki and Sigyn.

It took me three attempts to complete this journey and mission. The first time, I brought one apple and Sigyn fed it to Loki. I reasoned that if I brought another one, She would eat it this time, but She refused it again and fed it to Loki. The third time, I brought two apples and beer. I gave the beer and one apple to Loki and the other apple to Sigyn. I asked Her to eat it at the request of Her son and She did eat it while I held the bowl to catch the poison.

I found myself watching Sigyn as She ate the apple, watching age fall from Her delicate frame like leaves falling from a tree, exposing the miraculous, vigorous framework beneath. "Watch how you are holding the bowl," she kept saying in a firm but gentle voice. I found myself overwhelmed and awed at the significance of this lesson. The lesson is meaningful on a number of levels for me. First, it is a lesson about mindfulness and being "in the moment", being fully committed and focused on what you are doing at any given time This is a skill which I am currently working at improving.

Secondly, this is a lesson about devotion and perseverance. The poison will never stop dripping. When Sigyn moves to empty the bowl, the poison drips on Loki. Sigyn knows that She can soften this punishment, but for all Her love and devotion, She cannot shield Him from the pain of it all together. Some poison must necessarily fall on Loki as She moves to empty the larger quantity of it, which has been caught in the bowl.

And what is this poison, what is its name? It could be called many things but in this context of my lesson, I think it is called "constraint", a measure of the reduction of variety or freedom. A constraint dampens or reduces the effect of something without eliminating the thing entirely. A constraint simplifies things, focuses them; it is a check/balance response.

So Sigyn's bowl is also a constraint and a focus of Her power. She must focus Her attention on the bowl and how She holds it. If She were to hold it or handle it carelessly, Her act would be meaningless to its intended purpose. She must hold the bowl carefully and apply Her power to help in a very focused and measured way. She must match Her help to the situation in perfect balance and rhythm—otherwise it would be no help at all.

To me, Sigyn represents inviolable sanctuary, love, innocence, compassion ... all that which is worth protecting and striving for. In some ways She is the embrace of acceptance and love in life, just as Hela is the accepting and loving embrace of death. They are both Goddesses of sanctuary Who never turn you away unless there is a reason of your own higher good to do so. Sigyn turned me away a year ago when I asked Her for Her help. It was what She needed to do to best help me. It was wonderful to be able to show Her my gratitude for Her teaching in this way, by bringing Her the apples.

I asked Sigyn if She had any words or things She would like me to deliver for Her to anyone. She said something, which I think was meant for both of us and all whose lives we touch. The statement was simply "Love. Continue to pour your love out into the streams of the world." I interpreted this to mean, for me in my life and work, to persevere and strive to temper the desire to help with the constraints of thoughtfulness and mindfulness; with respect for the freedom of self-determination and dignity of others, carefully and compassionately matching the intervention to the need and never holding back from doing what is truly needed at any given time. I am grateful for the opportunity to be a useful servant of the Gods and to learn this lesson from Sigyn.

Sigyn's Angst
Tracy Nichols

The bowl is full again.
Can you see My tears through Your haze of agony?
Over your screams of pain can You hear Me crying?
The bowl is full again.
Does the snake ever run out of venom?
Will it ever run out? Ever?
Will it ever die, and take Your pain with it?
The bowl is full again.
Does Our Son speak to You, even though He's dead
Is He sorry that He keeps You chained to Your rocky bed?
The bowl is full again.
They said Your Children were monsters,
Ripped Them from Their Mother's arms.
The bowl is full again.
But I know how much You love Us,
Both Your Wives, all of Your Children.
The bowl is full again.
How dare They punish You when
They Themselves are not innocent of wrong doing?
The bowl is full again.
Why are none of Them being made to pay for Their crimes?
What nerve, what utter gall.
The bowl is full again.
It's been hard for Me, I confess,
To stay loyal, to stay true.
The bowl is full again.
I must be insane to keep doing this
Has My love for You driven Me
to have no regard for Myself?

* *Previously appeared in* From The Heart, For The Heart © *2007 Tracy Nichols.*

The bowl is full again.
My Children are dead, the One killed by the Other
And My Beloved lies here in agony.
The bowl is full again.
Why am I not angry?
Why am I not out there fighting for Your freedom?
Why can't I free you Myself?
The bowl is full again.
I've tried, I have really tried
But the chains are too strong,
Even in death My Son is strong.
The bowl is full again.
Please, Beloved, forgive Me.
I hope that My inability to free You
Does not destroy laughter.
The bowl is full again.
Do the People who remember You think less of Me
For not being able to do what I wish I could have?
The bowl is full again.
I tried, I really tried,
But all I could do was try to relieve Your pain.
The bowl is full again.
I hope I can be forgiven.
Will I ever be able to stop crying?
The bowl is full again.
I wish I could do more, so much more,
But all I can do is catch what poison I can.
The bowl is full again.
The Hag and I finally see eye-to-eye on something,
Because for You, We Both mourn.

Sigyn's Lesson
Sophie Oberlander

I first met Sigyn at Loki's behest almost seven years ago. Up until that time, I hadn't thought much about Her other than in passing as Loki's wife. Needless to say, when Loki first introduced me to Her, I was surprised to have her come to me as a playful child. I tend to be a rather taciturn and reserved person and it seemed at first that Her *reason d'etre* in my life was to teach me to find the sparks of joy that I'd long been ignoring. She soon became my sanctuary, offering comfort in times of my own personal darkness. That alone would have been an immense gift, but I never expected that she would also teach me. Eventually, I experienced Sigyn as the woman in the cave, an experience that left me awed and shaken; but even after that She tended to come to me as one young and vulnerable, eliciting my feelings of protection. Through Her, I learned to open my heart again. Through Her, I learned to value the less tangible forms of strength.

From my experience, Sigyn is largely ignored by modern Heathens. Perhaps that has to do with the reputation of Her husband or perhaps it is merely that there are so few references to Her in the lore. And of course, Her voice is quiet. She is not as pushy as certain other Gods and Goddesss. If one isn't paying attention, it's easy to miss Her voice. Loki adores Her, and I've often thought that to truly know Loki, all one must do is see how He is with Sigyn. She is a gentle Goddess but hidden within that gentleness is an immense strength that even Loki relies upon. She is His center, His ground, the one constant in His life. I have long been devoted to Loki and from His hands I have received many gifts, but the greatest of all was the gift of Sigyn's presence.

The Lesson:

You may think that I am not strong ... but I am. Mine is the strength of quiet endurance, of testing oneself and one's love to the limits and exceeding them. I am master of the ordeal, though few

would ever guess. I do not speak of it often. There is little need. I
know what is in my own heart and I do not fear it. My name is valor
because that is what I teach. Oh, it is not the bombastic valor of a
warrior returning proudly from battle boasting of his deeds. That is not
my way. My valor is the quiet courage of facing one's fate rightly. It is
the willingness to face pain and terror, to endure anguish and loss
because it is the right thing to do, without recognition, without praise,
without celebration. Mine is the gift of simply being at the center of
one's threads. Being constant. Being sure. Constancy of the heart is the
greatest of treasures, most especially to the Gods. It gives life within life
even in the midst of the greatest of sorrow.

That is not the only lesson that I teach. You warriors bowed grey
with grief, with loss, with hearts so scarred and wounded they seem
untouchable and cold, you would do well to seek me out. I nurture
devotion. I nourish the heart. I take all those things that are broken
beyond repair, shattered and discarded, and I make them whole again. I
value every scar, every broken place. They are marks of courage and
passion and life and love. How could I not value them? I see everything
that lies hidden in those dark places and I love them. I love the wild
passions so often and so early crushed, the fierce joy, the
inquisitiveness, the stunningly pure hopefulness a human heart can
hold. I nourish these things too. There is terror and anguish, immense
pain and even worse suffering in all the worlds. Even the Gods taste of
it in our own way, many times. It is part and parcel of each and every
thread ever woven. But to armor yourself so terribly against the pain,
that the flame of devotion I would have you so carefully tend flickers
and dies is not the way. Armored so tightly against the world, I would
ask you what it is you fight for? To be armored so carefully against life
does nothing but diminish the self.

I have seen many warriors coming to my husband's hall. They
boast and brag and hide their hurts. Their lives are filled with fear and
desperation, their hearts aching for beauty, for constancy for love,
though they would admit it not. I have seen men and women too so
caught up in the terrible roles that they play with each other, that they

have forgotten their own names. They have forgotten who they are and what is worse, who they once wanted to be. They are inconstant, with themselves most of all. They will slay a thousand dragons for someone else, or for a word of praise, but never turn to face their own. I value a warrior's courage, never think that I don't. I value their quiet pride in their own accomplishments, that centered knowledge that is so much a part of a true warrior's soul. It is not that I speak of. Rather it is the poison of false courage that eats away at the heart like a strange and deadly worm, that I would fight against.

That is why I so often take the form of a child. Even the most wounded reveal themselves to the playfulness and innocence of a child. I do not threaten. That is not my way. I am patient. But I wear few masks and none at all upon my heart. I have learned to cherish small things. I have learned to disregard nothing that the heart gives. Love comes in so many small and unexpected ways and it has the power to nourish and sustain. Nourish those fragments, however slender or broken they may be. Nourish them in yourself and in others and do not do that which wounds another's spirit. Great things can come from facing your loneliness and fear. It is often those slender, tenuous bonds of affection and love that provide the lifeline in that darkness. I know about anguish. I know about loss. But most of all, I know about love. Love carries with it duty, duty that often tears at the soul. But through honoring both, it is possible to find one's true self. It is a powerful thing when duty and love are twinned and that especially is the gift I bring.

Sigyn Bath

Jason Freysson

Step I: Make Balmy Water

For every pint of spring water, add ½ cup of coarsely chopped Balm of Gilead buds. Bring to a boil in a Dutch Oven and let simmer for twenty minutes. Remove from heat and allow to steep for forty minutes. Strain the water through a cheesecloth. Discard the herb and put the strained water aside.

Step II: Mixing the Bath

You will need a gallon and one pint of the previously prepared "balmy water." Mix together the following herbs:

1 cup comfrey
½ cup lily of the valley
1 ½ cup heather
½ cup orris pebbles
1 cup sandalwood, coarsely chopped
1 cup magnolia flowers
½ cup oakmoss.

Heat the balmy water to just below boiling and pour it over the blended herbs. Allow this to steep for thirty minutes. Add seven drops of sandalwood oil, five drops of lily of the valley oil, five drops of heather oil, four drops of magnolia oil.

Allow this to sit for six days divided evenly among six jars. Strain through a cheesecloth and use this bath as a Sigyn devotional act for six consecutive days.

Resolve
Silence Maestas

I would run to the hills to find you
Past the trees dusky with night;
Away from the town with its hurry and haste
Away from the hectic routine
To a place made sacred by your secret voice
Whispered in my most secret ear.

I would forget the struggle to hear you
I'd quiet the confusion and grief;
No comment or scorn would halt me
No dissuasion turn me away
From making your voice the loudest
Report in my quiet heart.

I would embrace the unknown to hold you
Be open to regret and desire;
Open to freedom and open to fright
Open to no-chance-to-turn-back
Released from options that don't include you
I'll stay by your side till the last.

I would hold the bowl to protect you
Guard you with hands and with heart;
Sacrifice my family and freedom
Give up my small cherished dreams
On the altar of love's resolution
I'll make my offerings to you.

I would face the fires to find you
Brave the heat and disaster;
In the midst of confusion and chaos
Between one age and the next

Is the one that I called Beloved—
I have no fear of your flames.

Eaten Whole
Silence Maestas

Let me lay a feast, Beloved,
a spread fit for a king,
a course progression from birth to death
to satisfy a rollicking hunger.
My days will roll across your tongue, tangy
and flavored with breath.
Appetizers, tapas, a splendid array
of time together, the weeks as garnish
on a platter of seasons and years.
Savor the menu, Beloved,
enjoy each mouthful of me;
my life is served up whole, Beloved,
and the salt tang of tears fill your glass.
Sample my confusion and heartache,
fill your belly with love; my dreams
a gumbo of ambition and heat,
a stew of passion and spice.
When you've had your fill, now satisfied
you lick your lips and sigh;
    with sideways glace you smile at me,
    "what's for dessert, my dear?"
With my dying breath you wipe your lips -
this chef is heartily pleased—
it gives me pleasure to serve you, Beloved,
because you've eaten me whole.

Loki and Sigyn's First Meeting
*(as told to Galina Krasskova)**

I am no teller of tales, no great Bard of Bragi's get. My inspiration comes from Woden alone, but every so often, another God will whisper in my ear for a time. I, with my small talent, record these things as faithfully as hands and heart will allow, but I am an imperfect tool and my words are often weak for the task at hand. I beg indulgence now as I recount the tale that Loki has chosen to tell. It is what I have been given, and what I am permitted to share. He has left parts of the story out and glossed over others. Suffice it to say, Sigyn is his treasure and what he shares, he does with her consent.

This story begins before Loki came to make a home in Asgard. Oh, He and Odin had been blood-brothers for some time and He often visited the All-Father, even assisting him from time to time, running errands and carrying important messages. No one was as swift or cunning as the flame-haired sky-traveler, after all, and Odin often trusted him with secret duties. Loki was observant and sly and quick to note those secret things others would keep hidden from the All-Father, and these he also carried back to his blood-brother. The work appealed to him for a time, though it did not earn him any true place in the halls of the Aesir. Suffice it to say that despite his dealings for and friendship with Odin, Loki did not often stay in Asgard for any great length of time. Aside from his bond with Odin, there was little to keep him there. It was after the great war, when the hostage price had been paid and the Vanir had come to live on the Aesir's *odal* lands, that this tale came to pass.

Njord, sacral king of this bright tribe, had bartered himself and the lives of his children and future grandchildren for peace with the Aesir. He came to live among them as a hostage, though his kingship was never in question and he was given rank and respect among his new folk. He built a great hall by the ocean, and filled it with plants and

---

* *Previously appeared in* The Jotunbok: Working With The Giants Of The Northern Tradition *by* Raven Kaldera.

herbs and finely crafted things from the land of his birth. Here his children dwelt until they too built halls of their own. He was a peaceful man, though no less a king for it, and exile from the Vanaheim seemed small price to pay for an enduring peace. He was respected and well liked amongst the Aesir and many often came to his home to learn the skills of the Vanir—herbcraft, witchcraft, peacecraft and other things best saved for other tales. His children thrived in their new home and he was, more or less, content.

It was not easy, however, ruling a tribe in absentia, particularly one as passionate as the Vanir. Negotiations and political intrigue did not cease with the treaties of peace, and often he and Odin sat in counsel, two kings debating governance of their folk. Messengers went often between their two halls, long after fragile, woven peace became firm reality. It was in such a function that Loki first set foot in that bright and shining sanctuary. Years later when *wyrd* had well unfolded, He mused that had he known what would happen upon entering Njord's home, He'd have gone there sooner!

Odin had entrusted Loki with documents pertaining to some rather delicate trade negotiations with the Vanir. He was to carry them to Njord and await the other leader's reply. It was a simple enough task, but one that piqued Loki's interest. He'd never been inside the Vanic King's home and had heard tales of its beauty. Vanic architecture tended to be wide and spacious, light and organic in contrast to the more elaborate structures of the Aesir. The Sky-Traveller had an eye for beauty of all kinds and looked upon this particular task as an adventure, a chance to feed that aesthetic desire. Arriving in the hostage-king's lands, it was as if He had left Asgard altogether. The hall was best approached along a stretch of beach, and the smell of the sea, the salty air, the crying of the gulls and the chill of the water which permeated every breath was a welcome change from the often stultifying rigor of Asgard's halls. Further, the Vanir bore Loki no particular ill will; they had not the ages-old hostility with the Jotun tribes that so poisoned many interactions with the Aesir. He was often treated hospitably in their halls, and this day was no different. He was shown into an expansive indoor garden and told, with courtesy and apologies, that it would be a bit of time before Njord could see him. He turned down the offer of food or drink and decided instead to wander beneath the skylight, exploring the unfamiliar plants and flowers.

Loki walked amongst the plants and small trees, herbs and colorful flowers hearing a fountain somewhere in the background, slowly feeling himself relax. He could understand why folk tended to gather at this hall; it was a peaceful, relaxing place, and he thought it beneficial that this man had come to the Aesir. He had just lifted his nose from some glorious crimson flower when he heard a squeak and saw a small form ducking behind a bright, flowering bush. Curious as only the god of mischief could be, he decided to investigate and found a small upturned basket of sewing on the ground and a few scattered flowers. Grinning, Loki crept around behind the bush only to see the figure darting off again, and laughingly he set up chase. "I won't hurt you, little one. Why don't you come out?"

"No." It was a small, feminine voice from somewhere behind a row of flowers.

Loki chuckled. "Please? I am all alone here and have no one to talk to." He sat down cross-legged on a rock and waited, sensing that if he was patient and did not startle her, this little stranger would come to him.

Eventually, two little eyes peeked out from behind a fruit tree. He smiled at her and beckoned, trying to look harmless. Hesitantly she came out in full view and Loki smiled, a genuine smile, at the little girl standing before him. He says later that he felt dizzy and stunned and realized later that she'd captured his heart with that first, shy glance, but he did not realize it right away. With a little bit of encouragement, the girl approached him, looking at him with wide, worried eyes. She was slender, pale and seemed very delicate, though pretty. He wondered what she was doing there—she very obviously wasn't Vanir, she had not the abundant, vital power that flowed like blood through every

Vanic man and woman he'd thus far met. She faced him, twisting a bit of her apron in her hands. He just smiled gently.

"My name is Loki. I am visiting here on business. I like your garden." The girl returned the smile somewhat hesitantly and shifted nervously but crept a little closer. "I didn't mean to intrude," he assured her. "I didn't know anyone was here." He moved over and beckoned for her to sit, but she just blinked up at him owlishly. Finally, he asked her name.

"Sigyn. I live here." She told him softly.

"In the garden?" he asked with innocent eyes, wanting to see her smile again.

"No!" the girl giggled. "I got rooms upstairs. But this is my favorite place."

He nodded solemnly, "I can see why. It is beautiful." He considered and produced a bright purple flower from his sleeve holding it out to her. Her eyes widened and she squealed with delight as he offered it to her. She fingered every petal gently; it wasn't a flower she was familiar with. "How did you do that?" she whispered in awe, creeping closer.

Loki grinned. "Magic," he said, and beckoned for her to sit again. This time she did, curling her legs up under her, attention half on the flower and half on the strange man at her side. By the time Njord himself came into the garden to greet his visitor, Sigyn was giggling happily by Loki's side, the two of them wrapped in conversation. He watched them for a few minutes, pleased to see the little girl looking so happy. Eventually though, he cleared his throat to announce his presence. Loki looked up surprised and a little sheepish, Sigyn squealed again and ran to Njord's side, hugging him and then dragging him over to meet her new friend, babbling in the Vanic dialect. Loki was utterly charmed and it showed on his face, causing the older man some difficulty in suppressing the grin that threatened. "I see you've met my foster-daughter." He smiled indulgently at the girl.

Loki smiled, "She was kind enough to keep me company."

"He gave me a flower," she told the sea-king.

"That was very kind of him, and it is your favorite color too." He stroked the girl's hair gently. "But I'm afraid I must steal him away now. We have business to discuss. I shall bring him back later," he promised her, exchanging a bit of a smile with his Jotun guest. The girl looked disappointed but nodded, waving goodbye to her new friend, who returned the gesture, a small smile playing at his lips.

Their business was concluded amiably enough, drinks were shared, and eventually, he did get to see Sigyn again, if only to bid her goodbye. Over the next few weeks, his mind kept coming back to the child, flitting like a ghost through the Vanic king's gardens. He began using any excuse he could to visit, both business and simple social calls. It didn't do much for the Vanic ruler's salons to have Odin's Jotun blood-brother show up unannounced, but then Loki didn't care overmuch for those salons. He spent his time in the garden or on the beach, entertaining Sigyn, spending only as much time as was necessary with the others. Njord was always hospitable, if a bit smug as he watched the two of them together. (Had Loki thought about it, he might have questioned that smug look—after all, prophecy ran strong in Vanic lines.) He took to bringing Her simple gifts, pretty things that he knew would make her smile. She was obviously well loved and well taken care of in Njord's hall—other goddesses, particularly Frigga, Eir, and Idunna visited and doted on her—but she was very shy and he couldn't quite place the source of the sorrow that clung to her like a strange miasma. He asked Odin about her, but his blood-brother only got a rather sad look in his eyes and told him that was a question for Njord.

It was almost a year after he first met the girl that he finally questioned Njord about her. He'd visited again, on business this time, and acceded to the man's request to remain in his private counsel chamber. When Njord turned to face him, it was as a man and father, not as a king and ruler of his people. "You love her." He said simply. Before Loki, stunned and a little worried, could protest, Njord continued, "and you're curious about her."

It was all Loki could do to nod. "I don't intend her harm!" he protested immediately, used to being suspected of the worst by many of the Aesir. Njord simply waved him away,

"I know that. I see it, in the threads. You could no more harm her than I could." He sighed heavily and came to sit opposite the slender Jotun man. "But you're curious about her origin." The sea-king offered him a drink and settled back, eyes dark. "My son found her a few years ago, not long after this hall had been built. She couldn't have been more than four or five years old, a bruised, hungry, disheveled thing, crying in the forest. Ingvi found her when He was out walking. She tried to run from him at first but was too scared and too weak to get very far, and he has a way with children. He calmed her and brought her to me." He smiled a little, a smile tinged with pain. "We don't know where she comes from... I suspect she's..." he hesitated, searching for a term in the Aesir language that would not be derogatory. "Forgive me, a half-breed." He inclined his head to the man. "I've always suspected the child born of an Aesir and Jotun union," His mouth tightened "and abandoned as a result. She's delicate ... and too gentle to thrive amongst the Jotnar, and yet if she is indeed part Jotun, would not necessarily be welcomed by some of the more insular Aesir." He snorted. "I don't know. I could be wrong. She could not tell us. What we do know is that she was mistreated and abandoned."

"I asked her once where she was from and it made her cry." Loki whispered, looking stricken.

Njord nodded. "It was a year before the nightmares stopped. She remained very fearful. She's made a home here and I do consider her my own. She knows that," he said softly. "But some wounds are hard to heal." He sipped his drink slowly, eyes on the fire that crackled and danced in the stone hearth. "The women are kind to her, but ... treat her as something of a pet. I do not think they truly see her worth save a few like Frigga or Idunna. I know she has captured your heart." He locked eyes with Loki. "These Aesir, they betroth young. I ... cannot do that. It is not our way."

"I would not have asked," Loki said quietly. "She is too young." He looked away. "I would not have asked you until she was much, much older."

"It is written in the threads." He smiled. "Be her friend. She needs that. When she is older, we shall speak on other things. She has already informed me she is going to marry you." He grinned outright at the stunned look on the sky-traveller's face. It took a lot to throw Odin's blood-brother off balance. He did not think it untoward to allow himself the pleasure of knowing he'd finally managed it. (According to Loki, in private, Njord has never let him forget it either, something Sigyn giggles over.)

Njord was quiet for a time, "One more thing," He said slowly. "I know you have a wife in Jotunheim." He held up a hand to forestall Loki's explanation. "When she is old enough, you must tell her everything. I will not have her coming to you blind." Loki nodded, recalling again that Vanic ways were as different from the Aesir as the Aesir were from the Jotnar. "And build your hall in Asgard. She needs stability. I do not think she could tolerate being moved about." He rose and Loki rose with him, walking to the door. "My daughter is wiser than she seems on the surface."

"I know." Loki smiled, all the masks falling aside for a moment. "That is both a strength and a sorrow to her." He inclined his head, offering thanks to the man, leaving with lighter heart than before. He could only imagine how the meeting would have gone had it been with someone else.

Within a few years, it became clear to all that Odin's flame-haired blood brother was courting the young foster-daughter of Njord. It aroused no little consternation among some of the more traditionally-minded of the Aesir, though Njord protected the girl from all of that. He obviously did not mind that his foster daughter was going to wed a Jotun, and He only became angry once, when one of the men accused him of child abuse—insinuating that allowing Sigyn to wed Loki was the equivalent of selling the child into iniquity. The *shild* paid for that insult padded Sigyn's wedding chest and put an end to such open accusations. Njord's rage had been as great and as cold as the ocean depths and few wished to see him thus angered again. It was clear though, that no one understood the love between the two, and many assumed wrongly that Loki had used some Jotun witchery to win her affections ... to what end, they did not wish to speculate.

Loki never returned from his many travels without some small gift for Sigyn, and he even built his hall on the outskirts of Asgard, a gift to his bride on their wedding day. He found out, on that day, that she'd kept that first purple flower he'd given her. They wed when she was fifteen, though that is a tale for another to tell.

Violet

Elizabeth Vongvisith

is at the opposite extreme
from red, cool and slow like dreams—
the other side of the rainbow bridge.

You were, from that very first day,
fresh as green leaves, your laughter
colored from that gentle place
where I had not spent so much time.
But as opposites do,
you drew me, pole to pole,
my heart to yours,
your youth and vulnerability the matrix
from which would spring that seed
strong enough to resist the dying of the light
in that dark place we later shared,

far removed from the garden, you a child,
I only a young man, heedless of
the shifting balances which would make me,
the interloper, bound to you
by silken threads so fine and strong
a spider might have spun them.

And I was bound by you, your laugh,
that garden, that spring day,
your child's hands and your eyes
speaking of that far-off place
removed from all the blood and strife,
your eyes that drowned me in love
but never extinguished the flame.

And through all my alliances and enmities,

all other loves, through the memory of pain,
through the turning of the worlds,
I am your prisoner still,
swimming in violet, your face
forever the hidden radiant sun
glowing high above the surface
    of a stormy sea.

Stand By Your Man

As told by Sigyn to Sigrun Freyskona

Disclaimer: I am a spirit-worker. What follows here is strict UPG, and I believe they are the words of Sigyn, who sent me a request via Loki to write her story. I am not trying to "rewrite the Eddas", nor am I trying to make any of the Aesir look bad. I love the Aesir dearly, and there are in fact two sides to every story, graphic and disturbing as this particular one may be. I also realize this is not the best writing in the Nine Worlds, but I have tried my best to pass on Sigyn's message. Enjoy. Thank you for reading.

Memories haunt me. I remember walking through the great forest alone. I was cold, hungry and tired, but mostly I was afraid. I remember the curling taste of that fear on my tongue as sharp and acrid as the smell of smoke, or incipient flame. Most of all, I remember the fear.

When I was very small, I lived in a hut with my mother. She was volatile, often angry and she didn't treat me well. Many times, she would fling insults and curses at me, and sometimes she struck me, nearly always accusing me of being "just like the one who sired you." She would never say who that might be, but I gleaned that she had been driven from her home, her world, for the error of being with him.

One night, as I was preparing dinner, she lost complete control, pushed me against the wall and pressed a knife to my throat. "Half-breed! Filth! You don't belong with me, you don't belong anywhere. You disgust me." She was shaking and sweating profusely. I saw the gleam in her eyes, and I feared for my life.

"Please don't hurt me," I cried. I reached out to grab her hand which held the knife, and when I touched her there was a flash of light, brighter than anything I have ever seen to this day, and a deep vibrating thrum. I heard the knife clatter to the floor and ran as fast as I could. I ran and ran and ran, down the path, through the village, until I was deep in the woods. It was dark then, and the howling of the wolves was frightening. The sharp crack of every twig I stepped on was frightening. The rustling in the bushes was frightening.

I walked as far as I could go, then stopped a moment to rest. I found a big rock to sit on, and the tears came. Then I heard someone humming a melody I'd never heard before. The sound grew closer, and closer, and then there was a tall, lean-muscled man standing there. He appeared young, with long golden hair, and a kind smile. He was carrying a walking stick, and he was bathed in a warm, golden glow. "Why hello there," he said. "Are you lost, child?"

I couldn't respond because I was crying too hard. He came over and put his hand on my shoulder, and I began to panic; I was afraid he was going to take me back to my mother, or hurt me. Hopping off the rock, I screamed and ran. He chased behind me, and when I had to pause for a minute from my sheer exhaustion, panting, he locked his arms about my waist. "You don't need to be afraid, child," he said very carefully, very gently. "I'm not going to hurt you."

Something deep within me told me to trust him. No one had been so kind before. I choked out "Everybody else does," but I was starting to calm down.

He nodded. "What's your name?"

"Sigyn."

"I'm Ingvi." He smiled again.

Ingvi held my hand and we walked a little bit, till we came to a gigantic golden beast with an enormous snout and tusks. He looked at me, cocked his head to the side, and snorted. "What's that?" I had never seen anything like it before.

"It's my boar, Golden Bristles." Ingvi patted my head. "Climb on his back, and he'll give you a ride."

I climbed on the weird thing's back, and it snorted. We traveled for awhile, and finally in a stone circle, Ingvi drew some symbols in the air and sang, and in moments we arrived at a huge house by the sea. Seeing my obvious surprise, Ingvi chuckled to himself. "This is my father's house," he said. "You'll like him."

The next few days passed in a blur. Ingvi's father, Njord, introduced himself to me, and announced he would be taking care of me from now on. I winced, and looked around for doors so I could run away. I didn't want anyone "taking care" of me; I knew all too well that resulted in pain and danger.

Njord noticed this and tears fell from his eyes and ran down his cheeks. I had never seen anyone else cry before that moment. I knew I could cry, and I cried a lot, but no one else had ever cried for me.

"My child," he said, and held me close. Then we cried together.

Njord took me out to the beach, to watch the high tide rolling in. "You see that?" he asked.

"That's nice," I replied.

"That, my dear, is the ocean."

"Yes."

Njord turned to me, and I saw he was tearing up again. "I want to tell you something. Every time you shed a tear, it is your connection to the ocean. It is a reminder that you can feel, and that you can feel because you are a part of nature. You are a part of the cycles of life."

I have never forgotten that.

I was so scared when I first saw him. Then again, I was still scared of everyone and everything. My foster-family was kind to me, but not everyone was so kind. I knew the Aesir regarded me as an "outlander." I am, but outlanders are deserving of respect too. I wasn't used to strangers taking interest in me, least of all one as nice-looking as him. At first, I feared his mockery. What would someone so good-looking want with a plain little child like me? Still, he wasn't deterred by my anxiety or disbelief, chattering to me at every opportunity. Once I finally found the strength to look into his beautiful green eyes and saw a growing smile brighten his face in response, I knew beyond all doubt that he was mine. Time and time again he came back to my foster-father's house, supposedly on business, but I knew it was to see me. When he asked for my hand, I was not surprised.

The day Loki asked me for my hand in marriage, we were walking along the shore near my foster-father's house. The wind was stirring his flame-colored hair, and the sunset was making his skin golden, like Ingvi's was when I first saw him.

I had grown fond of this Loki character. I was already fond of him the first day I met him, but my love for him deepened with each passing day. Loki has an amazing sense of humor. In all fairness, Ingvi and Freyja are funny, too. Ingvi likes to make up silly songs, and do even sillier dances. Freyja likes to play with my hair and share clothes with me, although my taste is more subdued than hers. But it felt so different with Loki.

One day, toward the end of one of his visits, Loki stopped a minute to look at me, and the intensity of his gaze I have never forgotten. "You, Sigyn, are beautiful."

I couldn't speak. Loki cupped my chin into his hand and tilted my face up. "Beautiful."

"You don't think ... I'm a freak?"

Loki looked angry for a minute. "Who calls you *that*? Please don't tell me it's anybody in your family because I will chop them down and use them for firewood."

"No, Loki, it's not Njord and the others." I sighed. "It's my mother."

"Your...?"

I shook my head as vague memories, mostly intense emotions and the madness in my mother's eyes, came flooding through my head. "I don't remember much. I don't think I'm supposed to remember. It was just bad."

"Sigyn," Loki whispered, "I love you."

And then it happened ... we kissed. It was meant to be a soft little peck, but it turned into fullness of lips, and swirling tongues. Our bodies pressed together, and there was a strange tingling sensation between my legs. I was still young, not quite of age, but I was beginning to be a woman with a woman's desires.

"Marry me, Sigyn," Loki said, "and I promise you, nobody will ever hurt you like that again. I will give you joy like you've never dreamed of."

"Yes, Loki," I said. "I've known it all along, this was meant to be."

"I know," Loki replied. Then he looked down at his feet with a frown on his face, his brow furrowed.

"What's the matter, my love?" I asked, truly concerned.

"Sigyn, you need to know something." Loki looked up. "I'm known among your father's people as being something of a trickster, but I would never lie to you, my love. And that's why I need to tell you, if you take me as your husband, I will always cherish you, but there is another wife."

"Oh?" I had already heard the rumors, and such things are not that uncommon amongst the Vanir either, so I was not terribly surprised. After all, my foster-father had two wives as well, one in Vanaheim and the Jotun warrior-woman Skadhi.

"Her name is Angrboda. She's a Jotun, like me. She is the chieftess of the Iron Wood."

Now, I had heard rumors of the Iron Wood. I don't think I've ever been there, but with my memory being what it is, I can't be certain. I feel like I ought to know if I had been there, though, because even those in my own foster-family, who were usually more Jotun-friendly than the rest, made it sound like it was a very dangerous place. I merely nodded.

"She won't like this. I can make her promise to stay away from you, so she won't hurt you." Loki sighed.

I nodded. What else could I do? "I understand," I told him - and I did; and while his other wife and I would never be friends, we did carve out a certain mutual respect.

Loki and I were married before the Aesir. Because he's Odin's blood-brother, Odin stood by him and wanted to make sure Loki's wedding was done right. I was stuffed into a strange formal dress. Frigga, Odin's wife, fussed over the fit, as well as my hair, and the bridal crown I was to wear. She was kind enough. I had gotten to know Frigga well over the years and was fond of her, but it just seemed like a lot of trouble to bless people who loved each other and were committed.

I stopped complaining, though, when I heard the music. Ingvi had arranged for the best musicians in Ljossalfheim to come out and play the flute and fiddle and lyre and sing. He had also arranged for lots and lots of food; all kinds of meat, fish, poultry, breads, cheeses, vegetable dishes, and sweets were laid out. After the ceremony itself, Ingvi asked my new husband if he could dance with me. Loki gave his permission, and so I danced with my foster-brother, twirling around and around to the lovely music.

"You need to cheer up," Ingvi said.

"I'm happy," I replied. "This is the happiest day of my life."

"I can see it in your eyes," Ingvi said. "Please, Sigyn."

I thought I was happy, but I knew then I wasn't. Yes, I loved Loki more than anything, and wanted—needed—to be his wife. There was no problem there. The problem was that I was among folk who didn't accept me; whether it was Aesir, Vanir, some of the Jotnar in attendance, or the Alfar, I could feel it all around me. The Alfar, especially, radiated an air of disapproval. They had just been hired by my foster-brother to do a job, and while they liked Ingvi well enough, his strange foster-sister, with an unknown parentage and was another matter entirely. I was a half-breed, and I didn't even know who my father was. Somehow, I knew in my heart that I would be an "outlander" for the rest of my days.

When the festivities had died down and Loki and I were alone at the house he had built in Asgard for us, we sat out in the yard by the fire. He wrapped a blanket around me and pulled me into his chest, so I could feel his heartbeat. "What's wrong, my darling?"

"They don't like me," I said.

I looked up into Loki's handsome face, now frowning, and he nodded. "They don't care for me much either," he said. "If it weren't for Odin..." Then Loki stroked my hair, now unbound from its braids and running in loose waves over my back. "But you, my love ... it doesn't matter what any of them think about you, about me. We have each other. This is what counts. You are all that I need." And then we made love for the first time, and my troubles melted away with the pleasure of his body.

I had two children, Narvi and Vali - boys, and they both looked like me more than their father. I doted on them, determined to give them the happy childhood I never had. I indulged them in toys and stories and songs, and Loki provided the silliness. We were a happy family.

Loki was often gone for long absences. I knew perfectly well where he was—with Angrboda—but I never did get angry, because he always returned to me too, and to our sons, and never ceased in his affections towards me.

One day I was out in our yard with the boys, watching them play-fight with wooden swords. "Aaaarrr! I'm going to slay you," Vali yelled.

"No, *I'm* going to slay *you*," Narvi scoffed.

Loki appeared. I don't know how he got there. He was quiet enough when walking, but we were bonded to the point where I could usually sense him when he approached. Not this time. It was like he just ... materialized. He was dripping with sweat, and I saw a look on his face I had never seen before. He looked haggard, like an old man, panting. "Sigyn ... take the boys and go. Run."

"What's going on?" I asked, as I scooped the boys into my arms.

"Just go. Don't ask questions. Go now!"

I heard people approaching, the sound of horse hooves and war cries. Panic returned to me with an intensity I had not felt since childhood. I ran, dragging the boys along, I ran and ran and ran, blindly, knowing that if I dared stop ...

They caught us, though, eventually, Odin and Thor. We hid in a little hut, but they found us. Odin was robed in black, the bare eyehole that was usually patched exposed. Thor seized Loki and myself and held us, a thundercloud in his eyes. I heard a scream—mine—as I heard Odin's galdr, and saw my son Vali transformed into a wolf. He leaped on his brother Narvi and tore out his throat. Then, howling, he ran off into the wilderness.

The Old Man—Loki's blood-brother—stooped down, and picked up the intestines spilling out of my boy's body, with his bare hands. "What are you doing!" I shrieked. "What have you done?" I tried to strike him, but I was held too firmly.

"This is for Baldur," Odin said, very quietly. "A son for a son."

Loki was bound with the intestines of our son ... in front of me. As he struggled and shrieked, Odin looked at me, sternly. "He must be imprisoned for killing my son, but you don't have to go with him."

I looked back at him, just as sternly. He had put his eye-patch back on. "And do what?" I snarled. "Live here among you? I think not."

They bore the bound body of my husband to The Abyss, as they called it, tossed him so that he fell down with a loud thud. Then Skadi crawled down, using the rocks as steps. She had something in her hand, I didn't see what. When she came back up, Loki was screaming again, and Skadi had a satisfied, smug look on her face.

"What did you do?" I yelled. "Haven't you people done enough?"

She slapped me, hard, across the face. "*You people?*" She spat. "Don't you *dare* call me that. You don't know what he's done. You don't even know who you are. Weakling!" And they left, not looking back.

I heard Loki's screams, again, and knew I had to be with him. I made my way down the pit, trying to use the rocks as Skadi did, to guide my hands and feet, but I slipped halfway and fell down beside him. After I fell, the entrance to the Abyss closed behind me, and we were in darkness save a small torch in the wall, ever-burning.

A snake was dripping venom into his eyes. Loki screamed, and with this scream, the pit shook hard enough that some rocks were falling down. I suspect that those above the pit felt it as well.

The only memento of my childhood was a wooden bowl, from the night I was preparing dinner at home and my mother attacked me. I had slipped it into my dress before I left, knowing I would need to stop someplace and get water. I never parted with it. I took the bowl now from my apron, where I always kept it, and held the bowl above Loki's face to collect the venom.

"Sigyn..." Loki rasped. "You don't have to stay here."

I smiled and caressed his cheek with my one free hand. "Of course I do."

I remembered the kindness and affection he had shown me. The kindness and affection of the Vanir was just them being Vanir. They were just like that: they were frithful people by nature. Most of the Aesir scorned me. I sensed that the few that were good to me, like Idunna and Frigga, were good out of a sense of propriety. But Loki didn't have to be kind to anyone. He's a full-blooded Jotun. Jotnar are not the nicest race of folk by nature, yet he actually appreciated me for who I was. He reached out to me in my pain, and made me smile and laugh. He gave me the childhood I never had.

I saw the tears spilling down Loki's cheeks, and I knelt down to kiss them away. "Njord told me something a long time ago," I whispered.

"What?" Loki managed a weak smile.

And I told him about the ocean, and the cycles of nature. I told him how tears were a reminder that we are alive and feel, and all interconnected in that life cycle.

Then we were alone together in that terrible place for a long, long time.

Many, many uncountable years later, Odin decided to free Loki. "You've suffered enough," Odin said, looking sad.

"Have I?" Loki growled. "Have I really, now?"

"There's no need for sarcasm," Odin sighed. "And your wife is innocent. She suffered needlessly. Her only crime was being your wife and bearing your sons."

After cutting Loki free, he was too weak to stand, let alone climb up the Abyss, so the Aesir had to take him up. Loki didn't want to return to Asgard, or Vanaheim, and he didn't want to bring me to the Iron Wood out of fear of conflict with Angrboda. We built a cottage in deep woods, in a place whose name I will not say. But when I went to the river for water, I recognized the village across the way. It was where I had lived with my mother.

We never had any other children. Gerda, Ingvi's Jotun wife, secretly visited me from time to time, alone, both to bring messages back to my foster-family that I was well and to bring me herbs that would prevent pregnancy. I was sure that if we had more children, the Aesir would leave them alone, but Loki didn't want to risk it, and after what we had both been through, that was fine with me. We live a quiet life now, outlaws in the middle of nowhere. I know he's in pain, but he still manages to try to bring some happiness, and yes, some silliness, into my life.

Invocation to Sigyn
Pagan Book of Hours

Long ago, the Gods quarreled with each other,
And there were many chained, and many slain,
And those who moved the pages of History
Had their say, and their screams.
Yet there are always those whose screams
Are not heard, as History and its makers
Run them over. And so today we hail Sigyn,
Child-bride of Loki the Trickster who slew
The beautiful Baldur, son of Odin.
When Loki was scorned, you closed your ears.
When Loki fled, you followed.
When your children were slain, you cried out,
But none heard you save the weeping Earth.
When your beloved was bound by the body of your son,
And condemned to poison and pain,
You forsook all that you knew
And stayed with him, faithfully,
Doing what you could in a place of horror.
Lady of the Staying Power,
Innocent child-bride thrown into terror
Who survived, and grew stronger.
You who gather broken things to your breast,
You who understand the blameless
Forced under the wheels of circumstance,
Aid us in our moments of pain and torment
When we, too, are caught undeserving in the rages of the Gods.

A Meditation on Sigyn's Bowl

Fuensanta Arismendi

This meditation evolved as a consequence of putting out food and wine in offering to Loki and Sigyn every night, together with two small towels, one dry, one damp to feed and wash that part of Them that might still be in the cave. One day it occurred to me to hold the bowl for Sigyn for ten minutes, so They could have some small moment of peace as They ate. I have been doing this nightly ever since.

Hold the bowl. I never thought it would feel so foreign and yet so right to do so. We always think of serving the Gods by scurrying around doing things. Now I serve by 'just standing there'. I serve just by keeping still. My back itches. *Hold the bowl.* What does She have to look at as She holds the bowl day after day, year after year? Is Her Husband all She looks at, all She needs? Or does She sometimes look away, to dank walls and bare ground? Can She see Loki at all, or is it dark in the cave, endless night? *Hold the bowl.* If it is dark, how can She tell when the bowl overflows? When Loki screams? Damn, I'm crying and I can't blow my nose. *Hold the bowl.* Do They speak to each other? What is there to articulate when this endless choice to stay and endure says all that needs to be said? Does Sigyn think of Her children or has grief turned Her to stone, the better to give Her strength? No, I don't think so—She is the Lady of the Invincible Heart, the Goddess of Unyielding Gentleness. *Hold the bowl.* Time is going so slowly and I know I'll stop after ten minutes—what must it feel like for Her, who does not even know if this will ever stop, this infinity of stillness and grief and pain? *Hold the bowl.*

The monologue goes on, combining fervor and triviality. At times, one reaches a state of grace in which no thoughts or feelings intrude. All one's being is intent on simply being still, and being there. And when the ten minutes have elapsed, part of me is relieved to stop, and part of me feels exiled from my true place, the place I fear, the place I pray to be in because if They are in that cave, then that cave is my only home. *Hold the bowl.*

When I hold Sigyn's bowl, I sometimes put out some food and some wet and dry towels so that They can wipe the sweat and urine off Themselves. Sometimes I see nothing at all, and I am bored out of my wits. Sometimes I experience. My most poignant experience was sensing Sigyn take the wet towels and dry off Loki's bonds—Narvi's intestines, because it was the only way She could take care of Her son's dead body.

I keep a special bowl that I have dedicated to Sigyn for just this purpose and I use it for nothing else. It does collect poison and needs to be cleaned very carefully after each time because of that. Ten minutes seems like nothing until the weight of the bowl fills my hands, pulls at my arms. It seems to me that if everyone who loved Sigyn and Loki held the bowl for just a little bit, just ten minutes a day, perhaps She would not have to hold it at all.

Daily Meditation for Loki and Sigyn
Galina Krasskova

In her breathtaking book of devotional poetry for Loki, "Trickster, My Beloved," poet Elizabeth Vongvisith describes an image she received of Sigyn tending Loki in the cave. The poem is called *Hunger* and it speaks of how

> *Sigyn's arms thinned further by the day*
> *and Her ribs stood out like the slats of a fence...*[1]

It goes on to describe the terrible hunger that both Loki and Sigyn experienced in the cave and Loki's anguish as He was forced to watch His beloved wife slowly wasting away. For those of us who love Sigyn (and Loki) dearly, this image, the visceral, painful awareness of the agony of the cave, is almost more than we can bear to contemplate. Yet contemplate it we must if we truly wish to acknowledge and accept all that these Gods are and all that They encompass.

Certainly, it is a difficult place for me personally to journey to in my mind, in my heart, in my awareness—easily as difficult as contemplating Odin's anguish upon the Tree. Yet I find that it is to that place I must go if I wish to truly honor Loki and Sigyn and by doing so, I have the opportunity to hold for however brief a moment, a single, tiny drop of Their anguish. If I can do that, in whatever small capacity, if I can in any way relieve

Them of Their anguish for even the briefest second then it is worth entering into that pain. It is a difficult thing to see our Gods as subject to such wrenching, terrible anguish. Yet in each of Them, not just Loki and Sigyn but Tyr, Heimdall, Frigga, Freya, Odin ... all of Them, such anguish is there and the question comes upon the heels of that epiphany: what can we, who love our Gods do?

---

[1] Vongvisith, Elizabeth, (2006). *Trickster, My Beloved.* Asphodel Press: Hubbardston, MA, p. 38.

For me, that question was in a very small part answered by the anguished image called to mind in Elizabeth Vongvisith's devotional poem and from that new awareness, which laid me bare, I began incorporating a daily practice of mindfulness meditation into each of my meals. Because Sigyn and Loki starved, I began giving Them part of my every meal. Because He was forced to watch Her wither away in that dank, dark place beneath the earth, I determined to find ways in my meditations and devotions to honor Her sacrifice. Perhaps it is an overly simplistic longing but we humans are as children to the Gods we love and so, in this I believe in retrospect, it is the simplicity of the longing that nourishes Them.

The way in which I offer is very easy. At each meal, I immediately set aside a third of each item on my plate for Sigyn and Loki, consciously offering it to Them to nourish Them in the cave. I also commonly offer water or wine. I have been asked before why I offer food to my [ancestors and] Gods. The person in question could not see it as anything other than a waste as no one corporeal was eating the food. But if the Gods and ancestors are real, as those who love Them obviously believe, then it follows that food offered in love and devotion does not indeed go to waste. For me, offering part of each meal mindfully connects me again and again, repeatedly throughout the day, to the searing katabasis that forms part and parcel of Loki and Sigyn's existence. For a few brief moments as I consciously make my offering, I am there in the cave with Them. This devotional act, based in something so temporal, so physical, so obviously Midgard as food—the most essential nourishment, places me in the appropriate mind and heart space to shoulder the burden of my Gods.

Of course, there are times when I really don't feel like giving part of my food, when I am very hungry. I say to myself at those times: Sigyn is hungrier. And I picture Her in the cave with nothing but a bowl filled with poison that endlessly tortures the man She loves, a man who lies bound with the bloody guts of Their son, who was killed before Their eyes by His twin out of Aesir-induced magic. What is my hunger in the face of that? How can I not willingly sacrifice my food? It is by these small acts, simple things rooted clearly in Midgard consciousness that I have found one can expand one's awareness of the Gods and deepen one's connection. It is the least I can do for Sigyn and Her husband and if it relieves for a single millisecond Their anguish, then I am content.

When the meal is over, I discard the food. It is no longer for human consumption. There are times when I will go one step further. If I am cooking at home, I will often lay a place setting for Sigyn and Loki (and often Odin as well and sometimes other Gods) and serve them as I would any guest in my home, inviting Them to the hospitality of my table. This turns the entire meal into a ritual and I have found it to be a very potent practice.

Be with me, Goddess,
that I may be mindful.
Whisper to me of Your anguish,
Your hunger, Your loss.
May I never take for granted
that which nourishes my body.
May I never take for granted,
that which nourishes my soul.
Make me mindful, Oh Sigyn,
that I may be constant
in a lifetime of devotions.

In the Cave
Erika Jarden

Straining ever upward, arms like white willow,
hands held wide to hold the moonlike bowl,
grim she is, full of wild patience and silent
as the shadow, she attends to her heart's duty.

Acid-bitter hatred, drop by drop
fills the trembling void of the moonbowl
creeps up like stealthy evil
drop by drop filling and defiling its curve.
Slender fingers willow long burn as
drop by drop fills the bowl and overflows,
drop by drop the poison trickles down
quivering arms raised high, spilling death
and agony along her own frame, until
at last she must turn away to empty
the moon darkened with foul vengeance.

Loud ring the cries like frost-split stones,
the roar of the whale-road sings softer in the gale
than does He, bound to bear the wrath of those
doomed to die of their hubris.
His curses rend the sky, damned yet still shrieking defiance
to those who would not hear his words and now
cannot dare to turn away. Far away his kinfolk
gather, great of arms and mighty, thinking deep
on the justice of the gods.

Swiftly as soaring falcon she flies,
willow-slender grace etched as the steel is marked
by tempering blow and quenching oil,
to moonward raise the moonlike bowl

to catch again the petty hate, to wish
the bowl were indeed the moon
to catch the greater share of vitriol and bile
spewed forth from jealous hearts and
to grant greater rest to Him,
her heart. Again, upward flings her arms,
praying for the strength of mountains.

Acid-bitter hatred, drop by drop
fills the trembling void of the moonbowl
creeps up like stealthy evil
drop by drop filling and defiling its curve.
Knowing how the agony gathers there
willow steady she stands, trembling hands
determined as the winter wind to have their way.
Slender fingers willow long burn as
drop by drop fills the bowl and overflows.
Bearing with stern heart the ache, the burn
drop by drop, like melting snow flow her tears
drop by drop the poison trickles down
quivering arms raised high, spilling death
and agony along her own frame, until
at last she must turn away to empty
the moon darkened with foul vengeance
again and again, grim and determined,
heedless of the cost she harvests the
hatred and shame that falls blindly
from the gods above.

Does she wonder: how can they say they are Good?
Does she question: by what right do they call Him evil?

Skalds did not ask her story, nor sing her song.
Lost are the thoughts of faithful Sigyn

as she rose and bent like storm-tossed willow between grief and pain.
Louder than the ringing of swords,
brighter than wergild shine her actions
until Yggdrasil falls will they be remembered.

Sigyn: More Than Words...

K.C. Hulsman

One of the difficulties that modern-day practitioners of Heathenry are faced with is a dearth of information about the Gods and Goddesses. Many modern-day Heathens forget that ancient Heathen cultures were oral in nature, and did not rely upon written lore. While today there exist a number of historical documents (Eddic texts, sagas and kennings), these documents were, with rare exception, penned by Christian scholars after the time of conversion and were the exception, rather than the rule of how these tales were shared and passed on. These documents are thus very much documents of their time, are incomplete, and not necessarily representative of the religion or culture they are used to describe. Yet for all these flaws, the lore is still a useful springboard. Even for the Gods and Goddesses that we know little of, taking the time to think through what small shreds of information we do have, can be fruitful in understanding and improving our relationships with these Deities.

In the case of the Goddess Sigyn, we know very little. We know absolutely nothing of Her background. We do not know Her parents, nor do we know Her origins. What little we do know comes primarily from the *Völuspá* and *Lokasenna* poems found in the *Poetic/Elder Edda* (circa 10th Century CE – 12 Century CE) and is heavily re-quoted by Snorri Sturrluson in the *Gylfaginning* and *Skáldskaparmál* sections of his *Prose/Younger Edda* (circa 13th Century CE). In one instance, we know Snorri is quoting not just from the Poetic Edda, but also from the pre-Christian skald Thjodolfr of Hvinir's *Haustlöng* (circa 900 CE).

What we do know from these sources can be listed briefly. She is the wife of Loki; she is mother of Ali/Vali and Nari/Narvi/Narfi. She is listed as one of the Ásynjur (Goddesses of Ásgardr; whereas Æsir would refer to the Gods of Ásgardr) among deities such as Frigga & Freyja. The Gods turn Her son Ali/Vali into a wolf, who then slays His brother Nari/Narvi/Narfi. The entrails of Her son Nari/Narvi/Narfi are used as the ties that bind Loki to a rock left to the torment of a venomous snake that Skadhi has affixed to drip upon Him. Sigyn remains by Loki's side catching the venom in a basin in an attempt to spare Loki some of the torment, but when the bowl is full, She carries it outside to dump it. This is why some of the lore, refers to Loki being the burden or cargo of Sigyn's arms (because She holds the basin out to spare Him).

When reading this within the lore, it's easy to read this information, file it away, and move onto the next tidbit without the words ever really sinking in so that they have an efficacious effect or leave behind a visceral and heartfelt understanding. But if we really take the time to slowly go over this, to put ourselves into this moment, much about Sigyn can be discerned and this horrible ordeal can be made even more real.

Setting the stage: Loki's punishment

Some argue the reasons why Loki is being punished. There are three camps of thought: he killed Baldr and is being made to account for it, he is being punished for his true—though insulting—statements, or a combination of the two. While some may argue that he is punished for the death of Baldr, it is important to note that nowhere in the lore is he specifically called out for it. If we see Loki being called to answer for his crimes because he slew Skadhi's father, should we not also have a similar account present in the lore today of him being similarly and specifically held to account for the death of Baldr? While the possibility exists that perhaps such an account did exist but it, like so much of what pre-Christian Heathens knew, may have been lost to time. But when motivation of his punishment is examined through comparison of all the known lore, we find quite a dichotomy of belief, which suggests the motivation came down simply to the Gods not liking their dirty (but true) laundry being aired.

The Poetic Edda/Elder Edda is derived from a text known as the Codex Regius. The content of this text is quite strikingly similar to another manuscript of roughly the same time period known as *AM 748* of the Arnamagnæan Collection in Copenhagan. When the two texts are compared there are two interesting things are immediately noticeable. Foremost, that the stories in Codex Regius have been intentionally placed into an order which shifts cosmological time to that of a linear timeframe by mortal standards, and that the AM 748 has an Eddic poem not found in the Codex Regius, specifically *Baldrs draumar* which makes no mention of Loki in the death of Baldr.

By the time we reach Snorri's much Younger/Prose Edda Loki's role as described in the eddic poems Volupsa and the Lokasenna, are somewhat open to interpretation. The possibility exists within that interpretation that Loki manipulated events to cause the death of Baldr, or even admitted to it. Yet there are scholars who theorize that wide portions of the Lokasenna are most likely not derived from the pre-Christian culture it's said to represent. Some of the content on the Lokasenna, unlike many other poems, has yet to be attributed to an earlier work. History has proven that when Snorri didn't quote, he wrote to satisfy the Christian and political leanings of his employer and audience. While this can at this time be neither proven nor denied, it certainly something to be cognizant of when examining this lore. But, if we examine Saxo Grammaticus's Gesta Danorum (which predates Snorri's Edda) the blame on Baldr's death rests solely on the shoulders of Hod.

A love and grief that is bound in torment

Usually when people look at this section of lore, the binding of Loki, they focus on the flame-haired God himself, and only note His wife and the death of His sons as a footnote to the tale. But try instead to approach this story with human emotion. Put yourself in Sigyn's place. This is a story of such great tragedy and grief. Here we have Sigyn, whose husband Loki is punished quite horrifically by the Gods, and seemingly for only speaking the truth by airing the Gods dirty laundry.

The Gods do more than punish Loki, They punish His entire family; They make Them all suffer. They pervert the one son,

stripping Him of His humanity[1] and transforming Him into a wolf
knowing only the wolf's hunger, and leave Him to savagely slay the
other child. A wolf's preferred means of attack is by claw and teeth;
they habitually go for the weak tissue of the neck, ripping out the
throat. While we have no clear description of this in the lore, I think
it's reasonable to assume that this is how Ali/Vali killed his brother
Nari/Narvi/Narfi. Oh to be a mother, can you imagine the pain of
knowing your children were harmed so? That the one became kinslayer
of the other?

But then the Gods aren't satisfied there; in fact the brutal
mistreatment of Loki and Sigyn's sons is but phase one to make Loki
suffer. Next, at some point after Vali has sated His bloodlust, with His
teeth, mouth, claws and belly full of the blood and flesh and sweet
organs of His brother, the Gods take the body back, retrieve the
entrails of Narvi and use that to bind Loki to a rock. While He writhes
in agony, He remains fettered by perverted familial bonds, bonds that
will go fetid, that will rot; the nauseating smell of unprocessed food
and not-yet-eliminated waste flowering the place of His torment. The
smell of death burned into His nostrils over the hours and days He lay
there. Maggots no doubt were attracted by the smell, laid their eggs,
feasted and swarmed into life from the remains. [2]

While Loki lays bound by the entrails of His son, He lays bound
beneath a serpent, which the Goddess Skadhi set so that the snake's
venom would drip upon the prone Loki. According to the lore, when

---

[1] Humanity is defined here as the ability to allow reason to overcome instinct.

[2] The rotting entrails and Loki's writhing is what no doubt eventually enabled Loki to break free.
One could argue that surely the Gods knew that this sort of punishment would make Loki mighty
angry and He'd want some vengeance when He got free. Would They not have derived some
better form of restraint? Were Our Gods really this short-sighted? If as some scholars theorize
parts of the Lokasenna were invented wholesale for the sake of a Christian audience, this too
certainly follows. Snorri's Edda is infused with an euherimistic process intent on changing the pre-
Christian Gods into little more than extraordinary men who had tall tales spun about them. Do
not the events of Ragnarok (and what would set those events into motion), prove to a Christian
audience that there is only one God, and all other Gods will die out and be defeated before him?
Snorri's own Edda states that Thor is descendant, not of a god, a dwarf, an elf or even a giant, but
rather from Agamemnon, who was a classic Greek hero.

Sigyn was not there to catch the venom in Her bowl, He thrashed and writhed and that was the source of the earthquakes that shook the world. If it caused that much pain, the venom must have been like having a high concentration of hydrochloric (or some other form of) acid dripped upon sensitive flesh.

And in this not-so-quaint tableau, we have an image of Sigyn as a mother of two, now newly and traumatically bereaved from Her children. Her husband is imprisoned, punished cruelly by Her peers[3] and bound by the entrails of Her dead son, slain by Her other son. For all this grief, for all this pain She does not leave her husband's side, She will not abandon Loki. The strength it takes to stay by His side is a mark of Her character. But the determination if takes to spare Her husband any pain, is greater still. If the venom burns Loki with acid like torment eating and searing into His flesh. She must be waiting, even with muscles screaming in protest at being held aloft so long, at holding a bowl for so long while exhaustion and grief gnaw at Her very being, making Her body tremble. She waits. She no doubt must wait for the absolute last moment to take the vessel away to dump it; no doubt the venom burns and sloshes against Her hands as She pours it out.

This horrible agony is Hers. She knows a grief like no other, and yet in such great pain, it could not be there if She did not also have such great love. Love for Her husband, love for Her sons. At times She no doubt tries not to cry, knowing it is but another torment to add to Her husband, but the grief must overwhelm and the tears and sobs must come. How could it not in a room where Her husband lies tormented, with the repugnant odor of Her son's remains?

I challenge you to think on this, to place yourself in Sigyn's position, to ask yourself "If this had happened to me what would I be feeling?" While you meditate on this, I challenge you to take up a large bowl filled to the brim with water, your arms outstretched before you

---

[3] And no doubt these peers also represent those whom she has shared meals with, exchanged gifts with, and played host or guest to. Peers who no doubt had children in some cases who played with her sons, who now have killed her sons?

as you hold this vessel for just a mere thirty minutes. This exercise is but a finite, infinitesimal commitment to a Goddess who spent endless hours of torment staying by the side of the husband whom She loved.

Loki gets a lot of attention within Heathenry, He is either the God people abhor and like to pretend doesn't exist, the one cautiously honored just so He doesn't come calling, or sincerely loved. Yet Sigyn is for the most part overlooked. Few honor Her. Few speak of Her. And as much as She is overlooked, Her sons are overlooked more still. We know nothing of Them, except for the fact that They are Her sons and the manner of their death. In many ancient cultures, the worse punishment you could inflict on someone, was to take away their name. Has not history taken away Her sons from us? We may have Their name, we may have the grisly details of Their death, but we know nothing of who They were and how They lived. I challenge you to try to find Them and know Them.

I have long found that Sigyn is a Goddess who mothers and wives can identify with. She is also an excellent Goddess to turn to when you are dealing with someone you care about with long term health concerns. She can be a bulwark of both strength and compassion as you nurse your child through leukemia, as you try to make a sibling comfortable in her dying days, as you encourage your spouse who has a long road to recovery coupled with years of painful rehabilitation before him. She can bring the gentle and comforting touch of a mother to a small child in need of someone to chase away the nightmares, to kiss away a boo-boo. She is One who delights in laughter, though her heart is filled with pain. She cherishes life, despite the pain-hardened cast of Her eyes. Her love, her loyalty, Her faith, and Her compassion are unshakeable even through earthquake and pain, grief and loss. We should all Hail Her name, and count ourselves fortunate that we have a chance to know Her, and be loved by Her.

A Group Ritual To Honor Sigyn

Galina Krasskova and Fuensanta Arismendi

(This ritual is designed to be done outdoors around a sacred fire.)

The Altar

An altar should be constructed with flowers and candles, and an image of Sigyn if one can be found (for the past two EtinMoots, we used a fairy doll, which may sound strange but Sigyn has a strong child aspect and in that respect, it was fitting). Old fashioned keys, stones and anything else that one associates with Sigyn is also appropriate. A pretty carved box, pretty paper and pens, and diabetic stickers should also be provided at a central point on the altar. One may also include an image of Loki. Any food offerings should be laid in front of the altar on cloth. There should be a blessing bowl and a drinking horn on the altar as well and libations should be present. Something should be placed on the altar to symbolize Narvi and Vali.

Make sure everyone has a copy of the call and response.

Hallowing

Once the folk have gathered, the officiant should take up a candle (or a torch if this is being done in a setting where such is appropriate) and walk deosil about the ritual space singing the Anglo Saxon *weonde* song (a song to consecrate and bless sacred space). For those unfamiliar with this chant, any appropriate means of hallowing space may be used.

The officiant places the candle back on the altar and turns to welcome everyone gathered, explaining that tonight (today) we are gathered to honor the Goddess Sigyn. (They should take the time to explain a brief bit about who Sigyn is if there are people present who are unfamiliar with this Goddess.) At this point, three people prepared to offer invocations to Sigyn should step forward. Determine beforehand who is speaking first and in what order the others will follow.

First Devotee offers her invocation standing before the altar:

Hail to Sigyn,
Lady of the Staying Power,
Lady of Unyielding Gentleness.

Hail to Sigyn,
Mother of Narvi
Mother of Vali
Beloved bride of Laufey's son.

Hail to Sigyn,
Victory Maiden[4],
Enduring One,
Pride of Loki's Hall.
We honor You, Lady, this night
And ask for Your blessings.
Hail.

(Devotee steps back to her place. She may light a candle, pour out a libation or offer incense before doing so, should she so desire.)

Second Devotee offers her invocation standing before the altar.

The second devotee should read Elizabeth Vongvisith's prayer-poem "Victory," also found in this book on page 71. It is quite appropriate to the mood of the rite.

(Devotee steps back to her place. She may light a candle, pour out a libation or offer incense before doing so, should she so desire.)

---

[4] This is the literal translation of Her name

Third Devotee offers her invocation standing before the altar.

(I was moved when first doing this ritual to actually lay myself out face down on the floor before the altar and then move to my knees where I continued praying. Frankly, I have no objection if a priest/ess wants to do this. I think it provides proper homage to Her and teaches those gathered the appropriate way to show respect to a God. So if the devotee is so moved, go for it. If not, don't because it should come from the heart or not at all.)

Because You hungered in the cave, we have brought You food.
Because You suffered thirst, we bring You water.
Because Your children were torn from You, we will mourn Them.
Because Your husband is so oft maligned, we will praise Him.

And because You, Gentle, gracious Goddess, are all too readily ignored and neglected, Your strength dismissed as naiveté, we will praise You. We will celebrate You. We will bring You offerings that all may know what glory rests in Loki's hall.

Then the officiant takes up the horn, filling it with alcohol and offers it to Sigyn with the words: "I offer this to Sigyn, beloved Goddess, Unswerving Lady of Gentleness. May it be pleasing to You." Then she pours it either into the blessing bowl or directly into the fire.

The horn is filled again and poured out, this time in offering to Loki with the words: "I offer this to Loki, Husband of Sigyn, mad, cunning, flame-haired God of desire, God of opening. May it be pleasing to You." Then she pours it either into the blessing bowl or directly into the fire.

The third time, it is filled and poured out in offering to Her sons Narvi and Vali: "I offer this to Narvi and Vali, children of loss, children of anguish, beloved Sons of Sigyn and Loki who have been neglected, forgotten and relegated not even to the realm of memory by those who should know better. May You both be honored and may this offering be pleasing to You both. May You never be forgotten again." Then she pours it either into the blessing bowl or directly into the fire.

The officiant refills the horn and passes it deosil around the gathered folk, who may drink, offering prayers to Sigyn or Her family. I like to pass the horn until the alcohol is gone (and usually at least three times), but gauge this by the size of the group. If it's very large, pass the horn once and pour the rest of the alcohol out in one large offering. Anything in the blessing bowl should be poured into the fire at this time as well.

Offering Box

Now the officiant shows the gathered folk the carved wooden box on the altar. They explain that this box is to be an offering to Sigyn and will be cast into the fire before the ritual's end. Folks should be invited to come up and write prayers, requests, and/or promises on the paper provided, which can then be folded and put into Sigyn's box. Physical offerings may also be placed in the box (the one that we burned at Etinmoot had an amber necklace, a large silver ring with semi precious stones, sacred herbs, and a few other items in addition to prayers and promises written out) all with the understanding that at the end of the rite, it is all going to be consigned to flame for Sigyn. If people want to make blood offerings that is fine too. Have a sharps container handy.

The officiant then invites people to sit and begins to tell Sigyn's story. There is enough material both from lore and moreover from Jotunbok and other UPG that the storytelling can continue until everyone has had a chance to approach the box. Ideally, the storytelling should be shared out between at least two people—it makes it easier on the speaker. I like to start by asking the assembled folk what they know about Sigyn and giving them time to chime in. If people have been having experiences with Her, it would be a good time to share them should they so desire. Keep an eye on the energy level and attention span of the people though and make sure this doesn't drag the energy of the ritual down. Use your judgment based on the gathered number of folk. It may be that telling Her story is enough. (Note: If the priest/ess has meditated with Sigyn before the ritual and been given an oracle, now would be the time to read those words. If not, then telling Her story shall suffice.)

Once everyone has had a chance to deal with the box, the officiant should take it to the fire and engage the folk in the following call and response:

Call: Hail to Sigyn, Wife of Loki

Response: Hail to Sigyn, Enduring Flame.

Call: Hail to Sigyn, of the Staying Power

Response: Hail to Sigyn, of quiet strength.

Call: Hail to Sigyn, Lady of Victory.

Response: Hail to Sigyn, Mother of Loss.

Call: Hail to Sigyn, Gentle Goddess

Response: Hail to Sigyn, Grieving wife.

Call: Please accept this offering Lady, with our prayers, gifts, wishes and oaths. *(The box is then placed into the bonfire.)*

All: Hail, Lady Sigyn.

Closing Prayer

We hail You, Sigyn, gracious Goddess of Loki's bower.
We hail You, Mother of loss and love and courage.
We hail You, delightful child Goddess
and devastating Lady of Grief.
All that You are, we shall cherish. All that You are, we shall honor.
We shall strive, Lady, to hold Your wisdom in our hearts
in our coming in and going out, in our rising and in our resting.
May Your quiet courage, Your ceaseless forbearance inspire us.
May it humble us, as You humble us, Lady.
May we ever be open to You and to Your blessings,
Lady of the Staying Power, Beloved Sigyn.
We hail You.

This rite is ended.
(People may disperse, continue to pray/meditate, etc.)

Sigyn and Loki love Their sons dearly and the loss of Their two boys is a grief that will never, ever heal. When Sigyn possessed a priestess at a ritual August 2007, Her first words upon seeing the altar laid out for Her and Loki were: "Where is the altar for our children?" The Gods do not forget and when They love, it is a terrible, fierce and enduring thing. Of all the nine worlds, Helheim was unjustly the richer because it held Her sons.

This essay was originally given in German to Fuensanta, and I have retained in parenthesis some of the original German words for greater clarity, in those instances where the English equivalent wasn't quite as accurate. –GK

Words Given To A Devotee by Narvi and Vali
(as given to Fuensanta Arismendi)

What do you know of pain, you who did not grow (*aufwachsen*) between a father who was a stranger and an anguished (*schmerzende*) mother, in polite disdainful surroundings that never thawed toward us children?

Did you grow (*wachsen*) with the capacity for shapechanging that was proof of your differentness, of your wrongness amongst the people you grew up with? Did you see in your parents' eyes the future in store for you—death and fratricide and still as a child have to pretend and pretend and pretend to be happy for Their sake, because since you were small, Their pain seemed harder to bear than your own dismemberment?

Do you know what it's like to cling to each other because each one of you is the only one that understands the other, and to know one of you will kill the other? You made us into a footnote in the lore. Was it for this we were fathered? Was it for this we were conceived?

And now, separated from each other, from the only source of comfort we ever knew, we hold to our torment as our only truth.

Go ahead, worship Them all—we will not bother you with our pain.

Prayer to Narvi and Vali

Fuensanta Arismendi

I who am owned by Your Mother and Father,
Live with the knowledge of the terrible thing done to You.
I shall not call it 'wrong' for it is not up to us,
Who are but foam on the Gods' wave,
To call it by any name, wrong or right.
I live with the pain I sense in You
And I live with the pain I sense in Them.
Both cut worse than any knife, and I can only hope, that as long as the
knife hurts me it may dip into You by that much less.
This is maybe the only thing I can offer You,
That is not a mockery, a travesty of respect:
My pain for a moment of relief from Your agony;
My rage for a moment of peace for You.

Lament for Narvi
Ayla Wolffe

Sweetest of sons,
Running through the springtime
With your chubby legs
And arms upraised to capture Sunna's kisses,
Laughter rising from your lips
And cotton candy kisses
That mother and father crave.
White pink skin that smells like clover,
With hair spun like silk gauze,
Strawberry blond a better balance
Between mother and father,
Never has been known.
Eyes as brown as currents,
Placed in your little boy face
Twinkling with the joys of youth...
Narvi I named thee.
We gloried in your presence,
We gave you every ounce of care
That parents shower upon their beloved babies.
Bringing you to glowing manhood,
Ignorant of the slurs said round corners
And near the closing (but not quite closed) doors,
Freaks, traitors in the making,
Never good enough to be invited to the feast,
Just the jester there to make others laugh,
Caper and cater to their demands.
Fix the mess and clean the stall.
We kept you to ourselves,
Shielding you,
Maybe too much,
We should not have tried to spare you this.
In the end did it serve you well?

It did not.
A hot knife through and through,
The burning rage that is vengeance
Cut you to the quick—
Now here I lay,
Bound by the very stuff that is you,
Feeling your weight upon me,
Not just the physical weight,
But guilt and shame
That you should come to this,
And I want to make it all better with a kiss.
A father's love is unreasonable
And I reckon one day I will make it all better
For my lost little boy.
Narvi,
Ever, were you loved;
Never has that ended.
I hold you in my heart
As you hold me to the earth—
I writhe not just in pain of fact
But seeing you cut down
Over and over in my heart and in my mind—
Never shall your name or image fade
In the days to come,
My son of the cotton candy kisses,
With the sweet current eyes.

For Vali

Mordant Carnival

Where did You go
When the deed was done,
Narvi's brother,
Loki's son?

Where did you take
Your sorrow and shame
Grey with grief
And the burden of blame?

Where do You dwell now
Wolf all unwilling,
Where do you mourn
Your part in the killing?

Oh Son of Ás
Oh Daughter of Van,
Far from Your garths
I wandered and ran.

Oh sons of women
Oh daughters of men
I'll never walk
Your roads again.

Forest and mountain
Tree and stone
Wild are the lands
I make My home

Lonely and ragged

Beneath wild skies
I hide myself
From other's eyes.

Now leave me be
Return to your own
For Loki's son
Would be alone.

Is there no gift that we can give?
Aye—if you make My brother to live.
Is there nothing to do that would grant You ease?
Aye—mourn for My Narvi, and leave Me in peace.

Wergild

(From Angrboda to Sigyn)
Raven Kaldera

In the accounting of sons, it seems,
Only One-Eye's tireless siring
Has brought him out ahead.

It was my sky-lads found him,
Wandering the heaths. They race the sky
Each day and night, my Skoll and Managarm,
In their deal with the Old Man, which I
Disapproved of, but they seem content enough—
Flight through the skies in exchange for keeping
Sun and Moon on track. It was they who found him,
A lone brown wolf, raging mad through the rocks
And lonely mountains, half-starved, tearing
At his own flesh. They cornered him, nosed him,
Herded him slowly to me. They had grown up
In the Wood, did not understand his fear
At entering. Are not all wolves welcome here?
Mother, can you heal him?
Mother?

But he was no wolf, not to start with.
What had been done could not be undone,
Save one small part of it, and that I did.
I taught him to take back his own body, at least
Some of the time, when enough sanity lit
That darkened mind. He had no training in the
Were-gift; his father's blood allowed the spell
To wrap him, but he was a sheltered creature
Of cozy hearthfire and fenced yard, he had no instincts.
We fed him, bound his wounds, my sky-lads held

Him with the warmth of their bodies.
We coaxed soup into his mouth when he sat
Staring at nothing, rocking back and forth.

Am I like him? he asked me one day. Not
Father nor grandsire, I knew what he meant.
No, lad, you are nothing like my great doom
Of a son. He is wrath, you are pain; he is at least
Whole in his rage, while you are broken
Like pottery on a stone floor. Hold still, I will paste
What I can with earth and spit and magic,
But some pieces are gone and madness leaks from the hole.

After all, I said to the air that was not my beloved,
I have some skill in mothering mad wolves.
I do not blame you, little child-bride; how could you know
The terrible fate our lover brings to his own?
And Odin pushed from one side, and I from the other,
And his own daughter from her cold kingdom,
Each with our own reasons. His women cried
For vengeance, for son and brother chained,
And I could only guess what One-Eye promised him—
You'll be all right, I'll see you aren't harmed,
You'll get away as you always do—how could he
Stand against us all, he whose secret weakness
Was the hunger for approval? No, he was lost,
And the girl-bride dragged into it, and now one dead as dust
And the other rocking at my hearthfire.

It was the least I could do.
I let him come and go as he chooses, feed him,
Give him warmth, as wolf or man. There is no healing
That my skills can give, so I send him forth,
A living memory of the ill-work that was done.

Laughing his soft, chilling, crazy laugh.
They let him come and go, As, Van, Jotun, all,
They feed him, give him a place at the fire,
Pretend not to show their discomfort—they know how unlucky
It would be to turn him away. He is the mad aunt
At the funeral, cackling, reminding them all
Of what they would not see. And when he is bad,
And the wolf circles and bites itself, my sky-lads come
And bring him home again, to what home I can give
Out of wergild for the one I did not intend to wound,
My sister-wife who threw away her home
The day that she walked down into that cave.

Grieving for Narvi

Fuensanta Arismendi

Nightly, Fuensanta lights a candle on Her altar and consciously mourns for Sigyn's children. She does this at Sigyn's request that Her children might be properly remembered. –GK

I never notice Narvi's arrival, when I grieve for Him. There is simply the realization of gentleness filling the room, of a somewhat wistful presence. Narvi has inherited from His Mother the invincible strength of the heart. This dead God Who once asked a shaman whether someone could bring one of Idunna's apples to Sigyn, tells me again and again: "Mourn for My Brother." Vali's anguish hurts Narvi much more than His own death, yet the one thing Vali cannot do for His Brother is to stop grieving. He rejects all attempts to anneal His pain and so, in a way, Vali involuntarily wounds Narvi again and again by this fierce torment for Narvi's death, a torment that has burned for centuries and will burn until the end of time. Narvi would, if asked, gently deny this causes Him pain, for fear of hurting Vali. In life, the Brothers were bound by Their love of Each Other, and now that love has turned to agony, *that* is Their bond.

To touch that grief means to be tossed from one pain to another, from one Deity to another. When Sigyn says, "Mourn My children," She does not mean us to think of Her grief. She is sending us away, to think of Narvi and Vali until one is overcome by grief for Them. So Sigyn sends you away, and you reach out for Narvi, and He tells you to mourn for Vali, Who in turn says you should do whatever Narvi wants but He, Vali, really wants to be left alone. Back to Narvi you go, Who grieves for His Mother, Who sends you back to Her children ... to touch that grief is to descend willingly into a spiral of anguish, a whirlpool of pain and grief that has no end and no resting point.

Loki and Sigyn do not mourn together for Their children. Loki asks some of His followers to grieve for Narvi and Vali with Him, and Sigyn asks some of Her followers to grieve with Her. Whilst this happens for reasons that are personal to Them, it may also be that a human being could not bear the weight of that combined sorrow.

As I never notice Narvi's arrival, so I never notice His departure. Mid-sentence, I realize the room is empty but for me. And because I do not know how else to serve Them, I follow the spiral again.

I grieve for Sigyn Who mourns Her children.

I grieve for Narvi, Who grieves for Vali.

I grieve for Vali Who is in torment for Narvi.

I grieve for Narvi Who loves His Mother.

For Sigyn,

For Narvi,

For Vali,

For Them all...

Three Wishes

Fuensanta Arismendi

There are three things Narvi wishes for. One is a wake for Him, the God Who was never granted an identity. Even when Narvi was killed, it was nothing personal, as though He were not worthy of being the object of any emotion, even hatred; and after His death, Narvi was forgotten by Asatru and Rokkatru alike, merely named as Loki and Sigyn's son, a footnote to Their story. Baldr was given a splendid funeral; Narvi was given nothing. Narvi wishes for a wake for His own sake—for His own rite of passage. And no, He would not like the pomp and ceremony of Baldr's funeral; what He wishes for is the kind of wake we give to the lost one we love, as we spend that gut-wrenching first night without our love's presence, wearing in and out of anguish, weariness and disbelief.

Mourn for Narvi. Not for Sigyn and Loki's son—that is for another time. Mourn for Narvi Himself, for Who He was and for Who He did not get the chance to become. Of the two Brothers, Narvi was the gentler One, resembling Sigyn and His maternal uncle Helblindi. There was always an underlying sadness in the young God, caused by the undercurrent of sorrow He sensed in His Mother, and by the Aesir's unaccepting, unrelenting, polite disdain; but He loved sailing and the sea, the tang and sound and sight of it, the relationship of give and take between the sea and those who use it without abusing it. Narvi learned much by observing the currents, the handling of a boat, fishing. He was the Watchful One, the Thoughtful One. Above all, Narvi loved—and loves—His parents and His brother. His strengths, like Sigyn's, is the strength of the heart. This is what little was given to me about Narvi. May people more gifted than I find out more, so we can mourn and honor Him fittingly.

Mourn for Narvi.

The second thing Narvi wishes for, He repeated again and again, as though to make quite certain I heard it: "Grieve for Vali... grieve for

Vali... grieve for Vali..." Vali Himself, however, wants to be left alone, though on the one occasion I was able to ask Him what I should do—since He Vali, wanted nothing to do with humans, yet Narvi was asking a human to grieve for His Brother—Vali's answer was: "Do what Narvi says..."

Grieve for Vali in a way that will not insult Him: rage for Vali.

The third thing Narvi wishes for, is that Sigyn receive Idunna's apples. Granuaile was kind enough to do this once. May all those who can journey and are capable of doing this remember Sigyn, and Narvi's wish. May Sigyn never lack for Idunna's apples.

I once asked Sigyn to show me the rune that best represented Vali before that day of atrocity. I pulled Othala. I had the immediate feeling Sigyn was showing me what Vali had been deprived of: His birthright. A few days later, I asked Sigyn the same question about Narvi. I pulled Othala.

Mourn for Narvi; rage for Vali. Weep for all the smiles They missed, for all the jokes unsaid, for all the food untasted, for all the missed awakenings and for all lost peaceful sleep; for all the sex and all the love They were deprived of, for all the children They will never have. Grieve for Their lost birthright.

Vali

Fuensanta Arismendi

Vali, Son of Loki
Vali, Son of Sigyn
Vali, Brother of Narvi, Brother of Vali
You who refuse all succor,
Tell me one thing: what should this human say to Narvi,
when she is asked by Narvi to mourn You?
What should this human say to Narvi,
when she is asked by Narvi to help You?
You mourn for His death. He mourns for Your pain.
I would help Your pain with my life's blood if I could.
And nothing can help it.
But You can help Narvi's pain.
Vali, brother of Narvi: what can I tell Your brother?

Two Prayers and an Offering

Fuensanta Arismendi

It was not until a very dear friend gifted me with Northern
Tradition prayer beads that I realized how much I had hungered for
structured prayer in my life, for the discipline and contemplation
inherent in daily repetition of devotion. The prayer beads also made me
realize how much I missed a "touchstone prayer," one that, like the
Christian "Our Father," would unfailingly anchor one to the essentials
of one's faith, no matter what may be going on in one's spiritual or
mundane lives. I did not find such a prayer anywhere in Heathenry and
so I attempted to write my own.

To Loki and Sigyn

My Lord and My Lady, my Beloved Ones,

May Your voice always be heard by those You call to You.

May I always love You, beyond mistrust or trust.

May my surrender be complete and voluntary.

Give me this day the grace of Your presence.

When I fail You, of Your kindness, allow me to make amends.

Use me and teach me in any way You see fit;

And deliver me from all complacency.

To Loki

I love you powerful, and I love You powerless.

I love You young as flame, and I love You decrepit as the dying ember.

I love You in Your beauty, and I love You in Your hideousness.

I love You in Your greatness, and I love You in Your meanness.

I love You kind, and I love You cruel.

I love You changing, and I love You changeless.

I love You sane, and I love You mad.

I love the force that drives You, and I will love You if You lose it.

Because I love You, show me how to love You.

An Offering

I have tried, again and again, to write a prayer to Sigyn alone, and I can't. Until I met Her, I thought the expression "a heart too full for words" was just that—an expression. Now I know it isn't. And so, my Lady of Unyielding Gentleness, my North Star, Goddess of the Staying Power, for what it's worth, I offer You my heart and my silence.

Joy
Fuensanta Arismendi

Every child Loki has fathered (that we know of) has had a destiny varying from harsh to harrowing, yet the one son He conceived was a child of joy. Sleipnir first came to me as a foal, probably because, as Elizabeth Vongvisith wisely remarked, "He came as Loki's child, not as Woden's steed."

Playful, like all young creatures, Sleipnir had such joy in His demeanor that it lightened the dreariest day. He insisted on odd food offerings and though I knew He was clowning, I loved to join in the game, offering the requested three small pieces of carrot ("no no no, that's too big!") and the requested three small pieces of apple ("cored not peeled") on a small glass plate ("not porcelain, harrumph!"). Twice I met Sleipnir as the Hunter's horse and He was so huge He filled the sky and was as iron-grim as a winter's day. Though the Hunter's steed is certainly one facet of Sleipnir's being, it is by no means the only one.

Unlike Loki's other children, joyousness remains Sleipnir's birthright. I have but vignettes to offer, scraps and fragments I was able to glean: a nudge on my shoulder blade that makes me turn around and sense Him playfully bolting away all eight legs a blur after having butted me; the way He looks at me with infectious joy from under a tousled mane that grows over His eyes; the way the room feels lighter, different when Loki thinks of Sleipnir: full of tenderness and pride; the picture Loki showed me of Himself as a pregnant mare patiently waiting for the foal to grow in the belly in its appointed time, standing in the sun until His/Her coat was bleached, shaking the flies from His/Her ears, playing the game according to the rules—for once—and for the sake of His/Her son. It may have been the most tranquil time in Loki's life, the one stretch of peace He ever knew. I have a picture in my mind of Sigyn, Her arms around the mare Loki, leaning Her head on the mare's shoulder, both faces tranquil: the woman's and the mare's. And though I know the chronology is probably wrong, I also know the image was given to me by either Loki or Sigyn.

Sleipnir is all too often simplified as the eight-legged horse that can travel between worlds, period. Yet He has aspects of His mother, maybe of His father (I have the suspicion Svadilfari might have been a God in disguise) and He is eminently worthy of worship.

Hail Sleipnir,
Son of Loki,
Prancing and prankster
Joyous foal.

Hail Sleipnir,
Son of Svadilfari
Implacable and inescapable
Grey as a winter's sky

Hail Sleipnir,
You who slip between the worlds
Defying description
Belonging like your mother
to all worlds and to none.

Hail Sleipnir.

Sleipnir: Noblest of Steeds
Ayla Wolffe

Striding through the nine worlds,
Eight-legged steed you are,
Wild as the wind,
Your voice carries—
Astride you Hermod
Wended his way to Hel's realm
Seeking release for the shining one,
You crossed the boundaries
Of life and death,
Roaring rivers—
Bringing back the messenger
With words for all,
Never a Wight would keep you
From tasks appointed,
Need-fires glint from your eyes,
Rime drips as froth from lips,
And sparks are lit as your hooves
Touch the earth.
Odin's steed, are you,
Striding in front of the wild hunt—
Progenitor of your own line,
Granni came from your loins,
Greatest of steeds upon the earth,
Who strode through the ring of fire
For Sigurd—
Who but one of your line,
Would have the heart to strive
In such circumstance?
Who would be so loyal,
To but one companion?
Untamable and yet affixed in spirit.

Loyalty not to be bought,
But earned.
Sleipnir,
Given of your own will,
Steed of Wod,
Striding the wild winds,
Over the nine worlds you fly—
Greatest of horses,
Son to the shifter of shapes.
Many are those who would possess you,
Yet few are those with the heart to know you.
Love the only mead which you drink,
Earning the regard of men
And gods.
We give thee hail for now and forever
Spirit of the ages.

Steel

Elizabeth Vongvisith

from one of Loki's wives to another

You have to believe
it is worth it: not just
the joy that makes you ache
all over, or the desire
that runs like wildfire under
your skin when he touches you—
not just these things of tenderness,
passion, linkage, love.
You have to accept also
the things that hurt, all
the losses, all the nights spent
wondering, late at night, alone,
where he is and if he's thinking
of you at all.
You have to accept, and in accepting,
grow stronger.

My family gave me this bowl
when I was wed. They cast it
not of gold, which would have been
the likely thing, but of steel,
blue-tinged and sturdy.
Others wondered at it.
I did not. Nor did he,
in the end, when he saw me
follow him with that bowl,
from which we'd drank at our wedding,
into the unhallowed darkness.

When I was not there, the venom of the serpent
trickled past his light eyes, down
past his temples into his bright hair,
to his ears, burning all the way.
It melted, bit by bit,
the gold ring in his lobe.
Gold doesn't last under an attack like that.
But the steel never failed.

You must not fail either,
sister, you who have loved him
and love him still. You must not
melt under the onslaught
of poisonous lies, worse
than anything he ever told
because the liars believe themselves.
You must accept, the way
a bowl fills, drop by drop,
and when you turn away to empty yourself
of all the tears,
find yourself still whole
and undiminished.
This is not an easy thing.
But it can be done.
For love of him, for pity, for anger,
for pride, for all these reasons and more,
you will become, as I had to,
the steel that does not give way.

And he will remember both
that you filled with love
and filled yourself with anguish
for his sake.

Loki has two wives—Sigyn, His gentle child bride, but also Angrboda, the great Hagia of the Ironwood, warleader, chieftainess and the mother of Hela, Fenris and Jormundgand. —GK

First
Elizabeth Vongvisith

We are neither of us young,
you and I,
and the water that passes under our bridge
flows with blood,
salt with tears,
yet hot as the day
your eyes first met mine.

And if I have committed a crime,
or many crimes
against you who was my first true love,
let that warm, gore-stained, tear-thick water
absolve me, for you are still
the quickener of my breath,
mother of monsters, wife
whose heart I swallowed
to bring you back from the dead.

The scars are real,
mutual and unforgotten, yet also,
I do not forget
that part of you stays with me always,
has remained and will always—
love underscores
even the battles between us,
love, terrible and alive
as the eyes that follow the unwary traveler

making his way through Jarnvidur our home.

I would not trade this, in spite of everything,
for your love called me, too,
back from the underworld
when I was as good as dead,
and I cannot forget
the warmth of you beating in my breast
even if it still hurts sometimes.

Hag of the Iron Wood
Seawalker

Her golden gaze is like a hawk's,
fierce over her cheekbones, one scarred
with the blade of battle, the other
tattooed with tribal bonds. More colors
crawl over her body, petroglyphs needled
into her skin, yet refusing to stay in one place.
I watch, fascinated, as the figures march
up her arm; I have lowered my eyes
from that fierce gaze. Her blood-colored hair
hangs about her, tied with bones. A handsome woman,
you might say, in that way that people do
when there is little dainty or feminine
about the woman warrior, and what with scars
and callouses on her sword-hand,
you would not think that she could turn her head
and smile, lazily, in a certain way,
and you would suddenly desire her more
than anything, than anyone, for that moment.

Not that she ever looks so at me, I am not
such a recipient of her gaze, but I have seen it
and seen the longing faces of those she eyes so.
One forgets, with the sword and knives,
with the chief's frown and the ragged
wolfskins, that she knows as much about sex magic
as does the golden Vanadis in her garden.

And yet there is pain in her eyes, long wrinkles
carve themselves across her forehead. She has seen
more death and loss than most, and held herself
tall and proud throughout. Thrice burned to death,

thrice arisen, her children torn from her,
fighting is what she knows. From her first years
as a young chieftess to her current day, she fought.
Never surrender. Never stand down. This is her strength.
Bones rattle in her hair. Mother of Death,
Mother of Destruction, Mother of Liminality,
Mother Wolf who hunts for her cubs.
She is the stone blade, the scent of pine and leather,
the shaman's circle marked out in tallow
and owl feathers, the old bloody mysteries
from days when folk hid hypervigilant in their caves.
She is the Lady of the Iron Wood, the keeper
of the powers that bred the world's destruction.
She is what she is, without apologies, without thought
as to what others might think of her. She simply is
what she has to be to survive the onslaught
of the terrible wyrd of her only love.

Whatever it is that Life gives you, she says to me,
Do not let it take you down,
until, at last, it takes you down.

Angrboda Incense

2 parts dried, crumbled oak leaves

2 parts pine needles

2 parts juniper needles

1 part spruce needles (or dried, crumbled spruce sap)

1 part viper's bugloss

1 part wormwood

1 part ground wintergreen berries

1 part agrimony (her favorite)

Mix and burn as you like, in honor of Angrboda. This can also be powdered thoroughly, mixed with 2 more parts red ochre and enough linseed oil to make a paste, and used as ritual paint to mark the body.

Two for Angrboda
Granuaile

I. Black Annis
She gives you a cage so you have a safe place to play
one with firm boundaries and lines
one that keep out those who would hurt you.
Not a cage of bars but a cage of dreams hopes and fantasies
of what could be if you are strong enough to live through all this.
Strong and brave and smart enough to survive.
She appears as terrifying and hurtful because that is a familiar face
and you take it seriously.
It gets your attention through all your emotional static.
Would you trust her, take her seriously, or feel safe
if she didn't hurt you physically and scare you?
Better physical pain and fear than the
stuff that hurts so deeply you'll never be able to pick out the splinters..

II. Knowledge, Wisdom and the Bed of Experience.
These are the gripping hands of Black Annis.
Knowledge and Wisdom are power, but not your power.
They are power over you.
Knowledge and Wisdom bring obligation,
the obligation to serve. Obligation is the price of knowledge
and wisdom. Two sides of the same coin.
For every ecstatic angel gazing at the face of God
there is a demon in its shadow who has been twisted
by the curse of knowledge and wisdom
and the burden of obligation to them.
That is why they always appear together in sacred places.
It is a warning. Gaze if you will, Seeker, but you will bear
the terrible mind-warping burden of obligation thereafter.
Knowledge and Wisdom are the fire of the Gods
that they let you steal when it serves them

and pass on to others as it serves them
until they decide you have served them enough for now
and they can chain you to the rock again
and leave you for the birds.
Black Annis is knowledge and wisdom itself.
She reaches in through the windows of your senses.
She grabs your innocence by the throat,
rips you screaming from your safe place
and drags you back to her bower.
There on her bed of experience she has you.
She pokes you, and scratches you,
flays you, breaks you open, turns you inside out,
spills your blood, gorges herself on your viscera,
and sucks the marrow from your wet bones.
Then she hangs your skin on her tree to cure you
so she, the knowledge and wisdom, can wear wear you like a skirt.
You know exactly what your place is then,
your responsibility, and what you owe her.
Your reason for being is to be clothing
for Knowledge and Wisdom, a skin for it.
You understand your obligation to them.
And you will never be the same again.
You will never be able to go home, you belong to her.
You belong to Knowledge and Wisdom
and She will never owe you anything for your pains,
your tears, your spilt blood or the sacrifices you've made for Her.
Those you left behind will mourn you,
and speak fondly of their memories of you...
but don't expect that from Her. To her you are a meal,
a hide, a suit, a window to look though, a hand to grasp with,
a tool which can be used and replaced.
Are you sure you want Knowledge and Wisdom?
Are you sure you are ready to pay the price?
Are you sure you can bear the obligation? Well, are you?

Angrboda, Mistress of the Ironwood
Ayla Wolffe

Mistress of Ironwood,
Sitting in the forest,
Smelling the fungus as it seeps
In the very marrow of your bones.
You work the Seidr against your enemies
Those who took your children,
Causing fear and anger
To be your lot in life.
Stirrer of strife,
Woman of mysteries,
Sitting in the depths of night
Muttering your curses
Against those abductors,
Against those who left your womb
Unfulfilled and wanting.
Angrboda they name you—

Wolf howls are your music
As they rise against the wind
Haunting in the winter,
Comforting against the loneliness
Knowing your husband
Rests in the arms of another.
Divided in loyalty
Needing to strive for perfection,
Teaching lessons through trickery
Loki walks away
Coming back at odd times
Leaving you always and again
Wondering when, oh when
Will the next time be?

Mistress of Ironwood,
You plan the day of your revenge,
And no one has sympathy
For your suffering,
Only scorn for the wailing
You send forth upon the winds,
A match to the howls of the wolves;
Ah to think, they are the only ones,
The only children to stay by your side.
Ride the wild winds, sing forth your Seidr
And call upon your guides.
Leave not your pain to fester.
Leave not your children wondering their worth,
Let them know the love of their mother,
And give forth your grief.
Angrboda,
Mistress of Ironwood,
Mother, Wife.
Live not your life, seeking always strife.
Look toward a balance,
Find solace, love and laughter
Even if but for a moment.
Uncertainty, but a ripple in the pond
See yourself reflected in the black sky above,
The storm clouds that gather
Give cry to your heart.
Angrboda, Mistress of Ironwood
Step forth and know thyself.
Let the world see straight shoulders,
Shining eyes and neck adorned with pale moonlight.
Adorn yourself with stars and be not bitter.
Simply be.
Mistress of Ironwood Forest.

The Hag As Mother

Raven Kaldera

On MotherNight, just before the winter solstice, Northern-Tradition folk often hail all of the various mother goddesses, or at least the ones from the pantheons they most often work with. Or, at least, their favorites. Some Rokkatru-oriented folks have taken to hailing Laufey, Angrboda, and Sigyn as the Mothers of the Rökkr on that night.

Laufey—the mother of Loki—is an earthy, mothering goddess associated with graceful trees. She makes soup. She speaks kindly to people. She is gentle even while being firm. Sigyn... well, there are probably plenty of wonderful things said about Sigyn right here in this book. Whether her shy childlike side or her tender nurturing, more and more people are being drawn to her as time goes on. Even folk who don't much like the Rökkr will sometimes hail Sigyn.

It's Angrboda who is the difficult one. She is the Hag of the Iron Wood, the Mother of Monsters who birthed rotting Hela and terrifying Fenris and the alien Snake. Those who don't like the Rökkr refer to her in words that suggest she is simply Loki's native concubine, and that his "true" wife is Sigyn, whom he loves, as opposed to Angrboda, on whom he merely sired a brood of freaks on before moving on to a "real wife" with, the implication continues, a "real life" with the "important" people in the Nine Worlds. The Hag is seen as an evil that he was fleeing in order to pursue that "real" life with the Aesir, a symbol of those backsliding tribal-giant ways.

It's true that the Hag is not sweet or gentle. If she thinks you're a weakling, she will kill you as soon as look at you, and would think nothing of eating your flesh, drinking your blood, and tanning your skinned hide for a garment. She is witch, warrior, werewolf, woman at her most powerful and frightening. She is the chieftess of the Iron Wood, the weird place full of trolls, werewolves, and strangelings. For most people, this is not anyone you'd want to call Mother, unless it were to fill that archetypal slot in people's heads labeled Bad Mother.

And, of course, she's the Rökkr goddess who has decided to mother me.

Well, it's not all that surprising, considering that I belong to her daughter Hela. When I grudgingly allowed that I might be the better for some nurturing and bucking up, it makes sense that She shipped me off to Her own mother for help. I was surprised at how helpful the Hag actually was. I'm the sort who mistrusts "traditional" nurturing—all that gooshy stuff, I've been known to say—and the Hag never pushed those triggers. For those who tend to be limp, paralyzed and self-loathing—what my partner refers to as the "whiny sack of shit club"—she's been known to turn into a ferocious drill sergeant of the "Get up and get moving, you worm!" variety. For people like me, who have plenty of willpower and for whom the roaring confrontational style makes us bare teeth, growl, and prepare to fight to the death, she simply looks me in the eye like the mother wolf that she is and says, "You're strong. You can do it." And I find that I can, regardless of what the obstacle was a moment ago.

Being mothered by Angrboda is like being parented by someone who is one part swordwielding sensei (think Skatha of the Isle of Skye who trained the young Cuchulain), one part barbarian queen who thinks you'd be helped by extensive tattooing and a horn through your nose, one part wicked witch who eats stupid children and makes love philtres out of toads, one part Morticia Addams-like priestess whose mysteries involve a lot of blood, and one part fiercely protective mother wolf. That's five parts, any of which might be too much for most people ... but I find that they suit me just fine. Like her daughter, the Hag pulls no punches. She is forthright and straightforward, and will tell you bluntly when you're being stupid, but where Hela does it from a coolly objective standpoint, Angrboda has more heat and sarcasm in her ripping comments.

I've seen her through the memories of her children, and I know she's capable of being tender when they're young and helpless—like any mother wolf—but where she really shines is when they're older, old enough to talk back and mean it, old enough to hold their ground. I've been a parent myself, and I know that there are many forms of parenting, as many as there are different sorts of children in different stages of life. If Laufey and Sigyn are balm and nest for the inner child, Angrboda is coach and teacher for the inner adolescent. I've always felt that my inner child, instead of being a wounded or withdrawn or trusting six-year-old, was more like a surly, defiant fourteen-year-old—and that takes an entirely different kind of mother to handle.

It takes one who won't let you get away with anything, but who inspires you to go it alone, without her aid. One who skillfully manipulates the power of "I'll show you!" to get you to achieve things you never thought possible. One who responds to your phobia of spiders by going out with you to gather specimens, spike their little bodies on pins and display them, watch them wrap and eat little flies, until one day your fear is entirely gone. (And you'll go along with it, or she'll drop them live and squiggling in your bed. She knows what's good for you.) One who won't take any lip, and will keep you in line when it's needed. A mother who isn't interested in healing your monstrousness, because if you're this far along and you're still a monster, that's not going to change. You just need some discipline, some self-control, and some skills to make something of yourself. Which is the best thing about the Mother of Monsters, after all. If she decides to love you, she will love you no matter how horrible you are. Unless you've taken leave of all logic, you can't convince yourself that you are too awful for her to love, because she'll tartly inform you that you don't hold a candle to her own brood. And she's right. She specializes in loving monsters.

We in the Northern Tradition are still feeling around to see what our Gods are about, what they specialize in, and there are few who definitively have "Will Work With Adolescents—Outer And Inner" on their cards, so far as we know. Mordgud and Heimdall, the guardians of gates below and above, stepped forward once as initiatory deities when I was doing a prayer for a child's coming-of-age, and we know that Gefjon likes teen girls, but Angrboda the Mother specializes not only in teens, but in problem teens. She'll take the sullen, the mouthy, the misunderstood, the violent, even the ones who beat up their peers and pull the legs off of bugs ... and she'll Make Something Of Them. She is the tough-love mother, who puts real love behind that, even when she's scaring the shit out of her little monsters. Because, sometimes, we need that.

The Mother of Monsters can also be remarkably supportive of people who are disabled and otherwise physically imperfect, so long as they keep doggedly trying in the face of their problems. She gives strength to the struggle, and good advice about managing the day-to-day problems, but the point is to keep you going, not to pat you on the head. The only folk that she seems to reject entirely are the weak of will; she seems to feel that they should be exposed, or made thralls, or at the very least turned over to the gentler Mothers rather than have them wash out of the Hag's rigorous regime. Yes, that's part of her dark side; she dislikes the weak-willed the same way that Skadi dislikes the weak of body. But as she wears her dark side in full view, it's not like you didn't have warning.

Unlike most people's experience of Laufey, Sigyn, Frigga, and most of the other mother goddesses of this cosmology (with the exception of Nerthus), Angrboda is the Mother who is perfectly willing to Talk About Sex. In fact, if you ask for it and she decides it's appropriate, she'll do the initiating, regardless of gender. She'll also initiate you into other, darker, mysteries, the sort that leave scars. Initiation in general is part of her job of mothering. She is very strong on ritual markings (I'm getting a series of nine tattoos across my back at her behest) and magical body modification. It allows one to see what Loki saw—and still sees—in her. I've always thought that if a deity had an astrological chart, and I was allowed a look at Loki's—which would never happen in a million years—his sun would be in Gemini, and the two-wife thing just shores that up. Two women for the different parts of his personality; the mysterious and passionate older woman and the adoring, nurturing younger woman. It's a Loki thing. To write off either of them is to misunderstand half of him.

The Hag also teaches leadership, especially of motley and non-homogenous groups who are likely to quarrel. She knows old shamanic mysteries, and as a skin-shifter herself she can teach that as well. She's not raising children, she's raising adults—strong, confident, self-sufficient, creepy, powerful, proud, knowledgeable, self-controlled, intimidating, stubborn, competent, sexual, magical adults. With a little blood on their hands and a lot of grim wisdom behind their eyes.

Hail to you, Grandmother. You have my gratitude, and my loyalty. I am one of your pack, Sacred Alpha Bitch, forever.

Long before Loki wed Angurboda, He was briefly married to Angurboda's sister Glut, upon whom He fathered two daughters: Eisa and Einmyria. It was important for this devotional that every wife and child of Loki that we know of be mentioned thus I was delighted to be able to include this prayer-poem from Elizabeth Vongvisith. —GK

For Glut, from Her First Husband

Elizabeth Vongvisith

You were
the beginning for me—
not the first to be taken
or to take, but my first love;
youth and inexperience
twinned with passion
formed, as it fell out later,
from the wiles of another
whose face was already
branded into my heart.

But while I still could,
I dressed you in soft skins,
colored the air around you
with magic and turned you ripe
and full with night's animal love;
your laughing daughters with hair
as brilliant scarlet in the sunlight
as your own,
as hers.

I knew I was not doing right,
and you seemed sadder, but even
in my wane and disinterest,
I saw there were better things—

a harvest of mighty trees,
delicate green leaves,
and another man bold enough
to take to wife the first love
of a firebrand whose heart
was pledged elsewhere.

And I knew too that they,
our lovely girls, they would be
better kept under your sheltering arm
than thrown into my wyrd to drown
as nearly all the others have.

So, my earliest hearth-friend,
I have no regrets, and I know
you will forever brighten and adorn
the wood of our kinsfolk
with your clear eyes and hair
like the fiery glow of sunset,
fire, embers and blood.

Jormundgand's Breath
Sophie Oberlander

It is to the serpent I pray,
Who girds the world
against dissolution.
I call it true:
Jormundgand's breath,
the thick fog rising
from the mighty ocean's body
that heralds Your presence
resting beneath,
the unknowable currents of
of Aegir's realm.
It is a comfort.

You cannot be known,
Serpent-child,
sired by Asgard's cunning and fiery God
on a Warrior of untold might.
But You can indeed be honored.

Jormungandr
Granuaile

My experience of Jormungandr has only ever been a blur of emotions and images like flipping channels too quickly on the TV. Nothing makes coherent sense, but every now and again you catch a word here of there and you get an impression of something. The lore tells us that the Snake encircles and binds Midgard as a kind of protective barrier and filter. But why? Why would Odin and Jor enter into a pact such as this? Why is Midgard so important? Hell, aren't we spirit-workers always trying to journey beyond its boundaries like there is something better or more valuable to be learned someplace else that we can't learn just by staying here? What do the Gods and Wights get out of ensuring the integrity of Midgard? What is Midgard's purpose? What role does it serve in the Nine Worlds other than being this place where these really fragile, short lived creatures exist?

Emotion, especially that triggered by intense experiences in the manifest world like SCUBA-diving with sharks and falling in love, is potent energy. Our emotions are very powerful and can move us to do things that we otherwise might not consider doing. Life is short in Midgard and there are lots of fantastic and wondrous things to do and see and experience here.

Just once when I was in the presence of Jor, I had the impression that the emotional energy in Midgard is like an engine or a battery that powers the grid for the Worlds. Would the Gods and Wights exist without us, without Midgard? I think so. Would their power be at all diminished if we ceased to exist? Probably not. But we are a potent reservoir of energy for them to draw on. They may not need us, but I don't think they want to lose us either.

Oh Jormungand
Ayla Wolfe

Ever circling about the earth,
Lonely in your watch.
When but a youngling
Were you taken,
Into the hands of those you knew not,
To find a fate long in the coming,
Long in it's fulfillment.
Far did you fall
From the home you had known—
Security soon to be a bygone memory.
The fires of the wildwoods,
The winds of the Ironwood,
That had wooed you to sleep each night
At the side of your dam
To be but a memory to hold tight to
Each and every night.
As you hugged the earth close
In your coils,
The only mother you would ever know again.
Seeking the warmth of companionship,
Seeking the sounds of life,
The rhythm of the cradle that had rocked you.
And what would find?
The sound of the surf,
The thrum of the lava deep within the earth's breast,
The scent of earth's loam
As it wafted to your nose—
And the sound of your name reviled.
The cries of your brother enchained,
The sob of your sister set far and away
From the light and the hub of the society

Of those who would never know
Would never choose
To find the brilliance of heart
Or of mind—
Because form over function
Was the order of the day,
The need for each individual to rein in
To obey—
And alone do you seethe
Waiting for the day when your rage might be unleashed,
When sorrow waits no more,
But a dream that acceptance could have been,
Would have been,
In an ideal society,
Which never has been?
And most likely never shall be.
Unless we can build it
Upon the broken dreams
That have been before,
Wipe them off, dry the tears,
Move on and know that the circle is unbroken,
That there's more inside than
Just scales and venom,
Go past the surface and discover,
Find the child waiting to become—
Oh Jormungand.

Third Snake
Seawalker

Up the spine,
The serpents twine
Or so they said long ago
In lands of heat and rain.
Kundalini, they call it, male and female
Rising up through the spine.
Yet some say that there is a third snake,
Both/neither,
More powerful than either,
That rises in their wake.

This I was told by the Tantrika
In tones of mystery; few know, he said,
About the third snake. That lore is gone
With only carvings on temples to let us know
What once, long ago, the yoginis knew.
The New Age music chimed behind me,
Yantras lining the walls.
And then, like a foreign visitor,
A dark face at the Swedish convention,
A pale one in the African Methodist Church,
Out of place, the Snake bumps me from behind.

You remember me. Said not in words,
But in a twist, a turn, a spiral of spine. Somehow a bit
Of humor is communicated—can a Snake have humor?
Is its life not all fish and water, stars and seaweed?
Perhaps that unseen smile is the inheritance
Of its laughing trickster father. Another turn, another twist,
That I can barely translate. But I know the gist:

That's me they're talking about.
And then it's gone.

Jormundgand, what have you to do with Kundalini,
And how can you live in my sacrum when
You live in Midgard's seas? It is a Mystery
I do not understand, and to bring it up
To the smiling Tantrika would no doubt
Make me seem mad, or at least too literal.
Are these things not symbolic? But no,
I've touched the Snake. It is too real,
Real as the snake between my thighs
Who I must take in hand now, as soon as I get home
And try to connect the one, somehow, to the other.

Spine/Tree
Sacrum/Root
Pelvis/Ocean
On the line
Between real and symbolic
The God/dess of Liminality lives

The Binding Ones
Michaela Macha

Odin:
Ill you kept your oath, blood-brother,
slaying Balder, my son!
Watch as I make a wolf of your own son,
tearing his brother to bits!

Loki:
Ill you kept your oath, blood-brother,
cruel foe to my family!
You exiled or killed nigh all of my children—
A wolf will revenge me on you!

Tyr:
Fenrir lies chained, as I fetter you now
with the bloody guts of your get.
Better such brood is bound in time
before it brings harm to humans.

Loki:
No hand you own for oathing or fighting:
Who would trust you, betrayer?
The wolf is strong, for he stands in a pack:
To Garm you will leave your life!

Thor:
I string these bonds to stones beneath you,
under neck, back, and knees.
Hlodyn will hold you heavily now;
Slow is time's passage in pain.

Loki:

The Serpent's coils will cling to you
before you fall to her poison!
How I regret regaining you Mjolnir,
which will kill my own kin.

Skadhi:

My father you felled, and the fairest of Gods,
and dared to brag of your deeds!
This snake shall spew its spit on you
and keep you eternal company.

Loki:

Better I liked your laugh, etin-maid,
when I was just bound by the balls.
Nor breathing nor dead has Balder been yours:
Go search the sea for his ashes!

Now leave, you traitors! Live in fear
until the day of your doom—
Your death will I be, Binding Ones,
when I break the bonds of the world!

*The following was given by Angrboda to Her mortal grandson on a day
of mourning at Etinmoot 2007. It was a day when first Sigyn and Loki and
then Angrboda brought home to those gathered exactly what it means for a
Goddess to lose Her children. –GK*

Mother of Monsters
Raven Kaldera

A mother wolf guards her cubs.
That, more than anything,
is what she thinks of for them—
keep them safe from all that might
eat them, until they are old enough
to be predators in turn. A mother wolf
loves her cubs, all of them, even those
who are unfit, who must be exposed
and left to die. Do not think that she
does not mourn them, even when she
does what must be done.
Do not believe that there is no love
for the corpse in the snow, the tiny
furred body laid to rest at last.

I could not protect my son.
His father's wyrd was greater still,
more twisted than any other thread
in the great tapestry, and all that branch
off it—no, even all that are wound with it—
become part of that great destructive wyrd.
It is my greatest shame, that though I fought
to my last breath, burnt and raging,
until I was ashes in the ruin, they still took him.
While the children of others were embraced
by their parents' love, ate at their warm hearthsides,

slept in their own beds confident
that they were loved, my son was caged
by those who would chain my womb
with my own son's breath.

Oh, Tyr and those who helped him tried
to train the pup, to bring him to heel,
Good boy, good boy, fetch that for us,
Fetch and carry, be obedient, don't bite,
And perhaps you can earn a few hours' grace.
A few hours out in the sun to be shown off
to those who hold you and your blood in contempt,
to sneer at you, to speak of you in venom-words
that your ears caught, no matter how they tried.
My son was fed, and trained, and treated not unkindly,
but there was no love. No love! How do you think
that one binds a heart that raw, a soul so wild?
Not with stern words alone. There must be love,
or all is failed. I am the Mother of Monsters,
I was made to love them, no matter their form and failings.
My son was no fool—he could smell the fear
on his caretakers, their relief when the day was done,
their false smiles. There was no love for him there,
save, perhaps, a little in old Tyr's heart,
and an old warrior crusty from the field
is no replacement for a mother who knows her child.
To them, he was merely an unpleasant duty
that must be done if the world's wyrd was to be changed.
If I could have reached out my heart to touch my son,
trapped there in that armed camp, I would have sent it
fluttering like a bird into his lonely arms.
Instead, I wept and raged alone, and he paced sullen
locked in a cage that grew tighter every year.

And after that, after all that, when he did finally escape,
what did they expect? Fools! My son's wyrd stood
on the razor edge of a knife, and they tore him away
to a loveless place, and sealed his fate. With one blow,
they thought to change Wyrd, and instead they brought it true.
The only one whose hands could have changed
that fate was me, and me they left impotent.
A son for a son, I said, between clenched teeth,
and waited out the smoldering years.

When he came to me at last, grown to a man's height,
lean and shaggy-haired, eyes like staring coals
burnt in his head, looming in my door like the dead
returned to life, I opened my arms to him.
Maybe there was a chance, one chance, one tiny hole
in the doom that had tightened around him,
and if there was one chance, perhaps it could be found
in the arms of a mother's love. There is only one way
to prove love to one such as that, on the ragged edge
of manhood, steeped in loneliness, and I did it.
I opened my body to him, where once it had brought him forth,
and let the others say what they may, I do not regret
my choice. But after he had arisen, I knew
that the last chance was flown, and it was already too late
before he reached my threshold. His doom had claimed him.
I knew what must be done. *Run, my son. If you must kill
Besiege the very gates of Asgard, and devour those
who wronged you, who have made you what you are.*

He never made it to those gates, of course;
he was young still, and had not gained his full growth
nor self-control. And I stood by, and knew,
and did nothing when they chained him, for what

could I do now? I had failed him, and the world.
His father and I, we sat silent in my hall
not touching, not looking at each others'
drawn visages, feeling every blow
as that chain tightened once again around him.
My son, my cub, sacrificed for all the reasons
which sound so reasonable when spoken aloud.

So there he lies, and all revile him, never mind
how he was made. There he lies, the demon
within each one of them, cast into darkness
that they might ignore the guilt laid before them,
the twin streams of blood that forever wash
their righteous hands. They have given him the burden
of being their demon, the embodiment of their inner hate,
and he bears it willingly now, for it is what he was taught.

I know what my son is.
I have no illusions about his soul, his hungers,
his ghastly maddened doom. But still I love him
with a mother's love, for I am the Mother of Monsters
and I love them all, no matter their flaws
or damage, so long as their souls are strong
as the love I have to give. And if my son goes
alone into the darkness,
I will not fail him again.

For Fenris
Granuaile

Footfall of a cat...

Breath of a fish...

The Duergar created a chain of six impossible things to bind Fenris, a chain so fine it could barely be conceived of.

A chain so strong that it could not be broken.

What binds us so strongly that we have difficulty conceiving of it and no matter how we struggle against it, it holds us fast ... a riddle? ... a kenning?

Fenris's chain is like six impossible riddles which if and when he solves them he will break free. He will swallow the sun. He will eat knowledge and wisdom and usher in a the age of Ragnarok. What does this mean? What is it connected to?

Is the sun wisdom, power, and all knowledge as the Celts and others have envisioned it, or is it simply what we think we know, what we small creatures think we see and understand in the so called light of day? If Fenris were to break his chains and eat knowledge, devour the light by which we think we see, would this plunge us into cold darkness or would it liberate us too? Would he be giving us the opportunity to go back to Peorth and Isa and reorient ourselves to the world via our more primitive and reliable senses? Would we suddenly be free like Socrates to marvel in amazement at what we don't know?

Would we, by this trial, learn who we really are and what we are made of? Would we in the darkness suddenly see the chains of preconceptions and misconceptions that bind us and hold us fast? Would we see clearly the ideas and thoughts that make us what we are? Would we see how our cognition and interpretations of our world limit us and hold us back? Would we see ourselves as we truly are? Or would we remain bound in the darkness only thinking that we stand in the true light?

In Celtic mythology the Wolf, called Faol, represents the shadow self one of the deepest and greatest teachers ... the one who shows us who we really are and what we are really made of. Though we may bind it in euphemisms, pretend that we do not hear it howling from within us, and rationalize away our visions of it staring back at us from the dark corners of our spirits, it will always be there, struggling to liberate itself and us with it. It is only when you stand in darkness that you can truly see light.

Learning to Love the Wolf
Tracy Nichols

The walk to the lair where He is kept is frigid. The land is frozen ice, muddy snow and slush, and cold that seeps into the bone. The wind howls constantly and there never seems to be any sun. Each labored breath freezes the lungs, each tear falling from the eyes freezes instantly and becoming another needlelike dagger of pain seeping in the cheeks. This world seems bleak, barren, depressing. Yet it has an odd beauty and peace to it that I suppose you need to be a certain type of person to understand and appreciate.

The journey takes hours, days, perhaps years. The wind roars and tries harder to be an obstacle making the goal unobtainable. It demands to know just how badly the seeker wants it, wants to know just how hard it can make the journey before the seeker cracks under the strain and the unforgiving cold. Pressing on, pressing on ... until at last, there is the blood mixed in with the ice and slush to signal that the Wolf is closer. Hot blood mixes with freezing water on the boots and clothes as the cave comes within sight at long last. Its gaping maw, much like the prisoner it houses, opens and dares anyone to enter. It sends chills down the spine but only strengthens the resolve to go on. No turning back now.

The blood comes up to the knees as the seeker enters the cave. The trail, the river, leads deeper into the cave. Deeper, and deeper, until the angry snarl comes out of the dark. A pair of monstrous eyes, golden and feral, blink in the twilight of the cavern as He stirs. The Great Wolf, Son of Loki, chained here by the Gods who became afraid of His power.

He is gargantuan, towering in the enormous cavern with His sleek black fur shimmering in what little light there is. His gaping maw, held open by a sword buried in His palate long ago, hold razor teeth that could no doubt slice into a person in a heartbeat. It doesn't help that they are being kept permanently frozen in that expression of rage and hunger that He no doubt had on His face when the Gods imprisoned

Him, the feeling of betrayal when Tyr tricked Him and broke an oath in order to chain Him. It is not just showing on His wolfish face, but it radiates in the very stone of the cavern. It sings in the blood ever-flowing from His mouth. Yes, the rage. The rage is His song. The air, the ground, the blood stinks of it. It penetrates into the bone, into the soul, and the soul is gripped by a crippling blinding fear. Run away, run away now, the blood sings, lest the rage consume you whole. The Gods knew this; that is why He is chained now, that is why He needs to be controlled.

Perhaps this is true. And yet...

In His eyes along with the rage there is also sorrow, and longing. Yes there is anger that has been, that should be, feared for it can be destructive. It can destroy all those around, it can bring the world to it's knees. Yet there is knowledge there that the anger is gaining more power the more it is chained up, for the rage needs to be allowed to run free in order to dissipate rather than be imprisoned to continue to build and build. The rage is not so bad either. For along with the anger comes passion and a wildness that yearns to be free, and it is seen in His pleading eyes. Like the wolves that are His children, He should be running free on the plains, in the forests, among the snowcapped mountains. He should be running under the stars, howling at the moon as one of His children chases it, drinking crystal waters from wildly flowing rivers.

He should be doing all this, yet because the Ones who chained Him cannot handle the rage that comes with the passion for life and the embodiment of all that is wild and free He is here chained, His days of roaming in the wilderness but a distant memory.

His sorrow too sings in the blood, in the stones of the cave walls. Yet He cannot weep for He has run out of tears, He cannot howl in grief because He cannot move His mouth.

So others, including the seeker, weep for Him. The seeker howls in grief and rage and sorrow for Him. The hot, angry tears fall down the cheeks and mix with the blood and mud and slush at the feet.

And finally the seeker understands what it is to love the Wolf.

The Killer's God

Raven Kaldera

A man who works with wolf spirits once spoke to me, troubled. "Fenris isn't a proper wolf spirit," he said. "He doesn't act like a wolf. My wolf-friends tell me that. He kills for sport and wastes the meat. He has no pack. He would devour anyone."

He's right. Fenris is not a wolf, or a wolf spirit. He is a God of Destruction who just happens to take wolf form. He is the Power that will take down the Universe. He is Hunger Incarnate, and no one is safe. If he were to be freed, he would immediately begin to devour everyone and everything in sight, starting with the poor sod who freed him.

And yet, he is sacred. And, further, he is worthy of love and I do love him.

Why? My reasons are both intensely selfish and intensely transcendent. His blood is in me, in my family. His wrath and destructiveness runs in my veins. There is a creature in me—I can't even say what form it takes, except that it is Predator—and he would gladly destroy everything in its path, starting with those I love. He would even take great joy in the destruction. He is capable of loving someone intensely and simultaneously, as a friend said jokingly, digging their eyes out with a teaspoon—and he sees no discrepancy there. And if you don't understand that, you don't understand Fenris.

But this is a part of me, this inner Fenris. I can't make him go away. He's there, and he's necessary. Just because there is no place for him in this, Midgard's sister realm of laws and rules and prison sentences doesn't mean that he doesn't have a use. he is my will to survive, my surety that no matter how bad things get, nothing can break me. People hear what I went through in my childhood and say things like, "Why aren't you dissociative? Why don't you have PTSD? Why aren't you broken?" It's because of him that I am this close to unbreakable ... but as a price, it means I get to live with him all the time, clanking his chains in my basement and plotting prison breaks where I can hear it at night.

If there's a Rule I understand, it is the Rule of Shadow Work: You must love all parts of yourself, unconditionally. You cannot go down to them hoping that they will change, or heal, or whatever. That's not loving them as they are, and they smell it, and they won't listen to you. And if I am to be able to love myself, I must love that part of me—the part that would thrill to the rape, the kill, the blood rippling in great pools across the floor and drenching my throat with its metallic rawness. (Yes, of course I've dreamed it. I live with that, remember?) So I begin as many people have begun, in many faiths: if it's hard to love yourself, start with loving God.

So I started with loving Fenris. If I can love this God of Destruction who embodies the sacredness of all that I fear in myself, perhaps I can then make the jump to loving my inner Fenris. A simple equation, but it started out with going before the Great Wolf and seeing him as he is, no romance, no chance of making him anything else. He is what he is, and he glories in it. He would eat the whole universe and love it. He would devour his own parents, who still love him even in his extremity. The first step was weeping for him, not out of pity, but out of awe. I could see his sacredness, and the predator inside me threw himself at his bars, howling in praise of his God.

Slowly, slowly, over time, I have been able to move from loving Him—even while I appreciate why He must be chained—to loving that part of me, which must also be chained. I've just got a lot more than six impossible things in those internal bars. I think that when mental health workers deal with people who present with unacceptable urges, they get caught up in the urges themselves. They are shocked, horrified, perhaps even vaguely titillated, and probably experiencing a surge of self-righteousness—why, they would never have desires so twisted and sick! With all the emphasis on the urges, they miss the fact that there are people walking around who have the same urges as Joe Serial Killer, and never lift a finger to one of them. The issue isn't the desires, it's what goes wrong in the self-control department. It's that the inhibitory mechanism is faulty. The magical chain isn't working right.

Fenris hates that chain, with all his might. So do I. I am also profoundly grateful for it, both his and mine. It allows me to have a life, to live, to love without it all spiraling screaming down the drain. Both sides are true, and both are sacred. And this, too, is a Mystery of Fenris: the chain is as much a part of his destiny as the possibility of the final bloody banquet. He is the weapon held at arm's length that you hope, with all your might, that you will never have to use.

I love the Great Wolf, even though I know him. Every scarlet, rageful drop of him. He is in me, and we are both worthy of it.

Once I began receiving submissions for Loki and/or Sigyn's children, it became very important to me to make sure that each of Them received some sort of homage in this devotional. For those of us who regularly work for and honor Loki and/or Sigyn, it's glaringly obvious that family and children are immensely important to Them. The following is a powerful and wrenching prayer to Loki's daughter Hela by one owned by Her. –GK

A Prayer of Gratitude
Dagian Russell

Thank You, Lady of the Cool Damp Places,
For showing me Your many faces, your many aspects
All the things You expect and all the things You Are.

Thank You, Mistress of Eternal Autumn,
For bringing twilight to my days of carelessness and excess
And an end to my faithless, aimless and self-indulgent wandering.

Thank You, Witness of Myriad Experience
For requiring that I grow in all ways, demanding everything
My pain, my discomfort, my successes and failures, my furious
    evolution

Thank You, Goddess of Wither and Rot and Decay
For stripping away my useless bits: my vice, my hubris,
And my fatalistic resignation, thereby cleansing my being
of detritus and denial

Thank You, Queen of Wholeness, Symbol of the Cycle
Visual and Visceral Reminder of the inherent nature of Existence,
For granting me a glimpse of Your Mysteries and Wisdom

Thank You, Crafter of Tools
For Your interminable Patience, Your ceaseless honing and

Your incessant Insistence, that such a specimen as I
may benefit from Serving

Thank You, Keeper of Souls
For Your transpersonal Compassion,
and generous seating at Your tables
Something for all, and All for Sustainable Cyclical Perpetuity

Thank You, Architect of Purpose
For Your Farsighted Vision and Benevolent Ruthlessness
And for Your tireless, Necessary and Wholesome Works

Thank You, Divine Domme
In gratitude I give willingly that which You demand
The works of this life and this death and this life again
So that my efforts may add to Your Great Work

For the Hel of It

Ayla Wolffe

Shrouded in darkness,
scent of rich earth.
You embrace to your bosom
the castoff of life.
Knowing what has been,
seeing what will come.
Champion of those who have suffered,
lost in the moments
when their hearts ceased to beat.
Lily of the night,
your white skin glows
under ministrations of Mani.
You walk with the slow knowledge
the death stalks us all
and eventually catches us.
The soul needs housed,
the body crumbles to dust.
Our lives books to be read
by those who will come after.
Dark Mother who accepts our pain,
hold our memory in your embrace,
though our flesh may rot,
our hearts may cease to be.
The nobility of spirit with which we lived,
will beat back the ways in which we die.
Know us, as we know you
and never shall either of us be forgotten.

For Hel On Walpurgisnacht
Ayla Wolffe

Older than the legends tell,
your halls glow gold in welcome
to the world weary traveler
who has no longer a place among the living..
Your grim visage softens
when presented with the face
of children taken before their span
should have come to pass—
You give what cold comfort
is yours within the bowels of Nifelheim—
Though your plate be not always as full
as that of others you share with an open hand,
and walk with the quiet grace of one who disturbs not
the worthy dead.
Those who have fallen to sickness,
those who have not the greatest of deeds to shine before them
you bring to your breast,
with compassion.
Those who have not find that which they sought in life
as they cross the bridge that brings them to your realm.
Quiet contemplation,
a life that allows them to retire from the labors
they strove so hard at each day,
And their knowledge is offered up when the Seidhkona calls,
not forced to be separated from those whom they loved in life
no not at all.
Hel do I name thee.
Beauty do you embody if one can but see,
the gliding gait—
Pale in the moonlight,
with flesh lily white.

But to look at other ways, the skin
might be dark and blend to the earth,
shy to the ways of the living,
happiest among the quickened dead who have such stories to share,
such heart in their passing.
You heal even the most broken of hearts among the living
should they but turn to you.
Working potent magics.
Turning the world round,
so that death is more than just a shroud.
It is a memorial.
It is you also,
who punishes those unworthy who have worked ill in this world.
Sending them to Nastrond.
Setting their final fate into motion.
And none could ask thee more.
For such a task is it that you grow in magnitude,
winnowing out those
who have no place among the many who seek to heal
in their passing,
heal from those things in life which they have done
and had done to them.
Ill-fated the residents of Nastrond.
Ill-fated they shall always be.
Hel, are you the weaver of the doom of the dead,
even as the Norns weave the doom of the living.
Your faces reflect the choices you must make.
And the face of terror is given only to those who must fear.
Hail to you, Hel,
I give you honor this day.
Come this Walpurgisnacht and weave for us
the veil that shows the way.
Let us speak safely with our ancestors
and let them rest thereafter.

Darkness Out Of Fire
(From Hela, To Her Father)

Raven Kaldera

As the eldest, I was the luckiest.
I had the two of them the longest, content
In my mother's hall—she like the hearthfire
That never burned out, but sometimes flared up,
He like the sun that came and went.
Two matched fires so hot, so passionate
That they almost made the coldness in me melt,
Or come close to it, on rare occasion.
I watched in silence as their love raged
And bloomed by turns; two so volatile could not
Dwell in quiet contentment, but I could see
How much they craved it. Each other's addiction,
Even coming to blows would mean pelting into bed.
They loved their children just as passionately
And loudly; I tumbled on the floor with my brother
And slapped him when he ate the bones
I had so carefully reassembled from the midden heap,
And our sister-brother, like a live toy, carried
On exploits through the forest. Yet I could see
In my parents' faces, the looks they turned on me.
They loved me, yes, but awe stood there as well,
And put a strange distance between us. When I grew
Chest-high, and my skin-swift form began to rot,
My mother told me to stay away from the kitchen,
But still stroked my cheek. You, father, took me
On your lap as you had done before, never mind the scent
Of Death, and kissed me, though your eyes watered,
And pretended it was tears.

I do not dwell on the day when our home was broken,
My siblings imprisoned, and I began the journey
Through cold and snow to seek my destiny. I knew
It was at least half your doing, that your tangled wyrd had
Shattered ours, but once I reached the gates of my true home
I knew that my own would protect me now. So I can forgive,
Save for my one act of vengeance, and that is over now,
And my brother's pain, the breaking of our homefire avenged.

I never inherited your fire. My blood hearkened back to Her,
Our first ancestress born of the sleeping icy mountain-sire,
She whose cold hand stirs the waters of the highest Well,
I was once her second daughter, before Death died.
Now I am yours, and mother to none of my body
But thousands of souls to care for. I sing dead babes to sleep
With love taught to me by a fickle trickster and an ungentle
Wolf-woman, yet if you were as they say, could this gift
You gave to me that I give every day to others,
Hundreds, thousands, could it be so strong and true?
You taught me how to love without judgment, as if you knew
That one day it would be my daily task, to stretch a cold heart
So wide open that it would hold a million souls.

Loki the Fool

Alice Karlsdóttir, 1982
Trad. tune: "The Old Orange Flute"

Oh, the great gods of Asgard are noble and free,
They are upright and forthright (as great gods should be),
But there's one in their midst doesn't follow the rule—
That sly mischief-monger called Loki the Fool.

He lies and he pilfers, tells jokes that are crude,
He's raucous, he's ribald, he's rowdy, he's rude;
He tricks and he teases, though he's not really cruel—
Just don't turn your back on that Loki the Fool.

In grim Jotunheim, where the weather is freezin',
He mixed blood with Odin (and who knows the reason?)
They laughed and drank wine, went on gay escapades,
Fought wizards and trolls, and seduced fair young maids.

Now some think that here Odin made a mistake
By tying himself to this impudent rake;
But I'll tell you a fact (though it makes scholars mad)—
If the Allfather likes him, he can't be all bad.

Poor Lopt's reputation is not of the best;
He gave Sif a clip job without her behest;
He lifted from Freyja her most precious jewel;
And Thor's got his hands full when he rides with the Fool.

He stole Idun's apples (which wasn't too nice),
Sired monsters galore and put Balder on ice;
And the gods all berate him for what he has done—
Well, gee, can't a boy have a wee bit of fun?

They say he's corrupted and wicked indeed,
'Cause he mothered the Allfather's whimsical steed;
It's not he's perverted or easily led—
Let's just say he's not very choosy in bed.

He tried to enliven sedate Asgard's halls
By tying the beard of a goat to his balls;
And they say that his tongue's his most effective tool
(And that's why all the ladies love Loki the Fool).

To the end of all Time he'll roam free through the land,
And all things stir and change at the touch of his hand,
And when the world's old and no fun's left in store,
He'll blow it all up and start over once more.

Now scholars and such say he's captured and bound,
But just look at the world, you'll see he's still around,
For to live here without him would be just too cruel.
Oh Loki, we love you, dear Loki the Fool!

About the Author

Rev. Galina Krasskova is a free range tribalist Heathen who has been a priest of Odin and Loki for close to fifteen years. She is the founder of Urdabrunnr Kindred in NYC, and a member of Ironwood Kindred (MA), Asatru in Frankfurt (Frankfurt am Main, Germany) and the First Kingdom Church of Asphodel (MA). Her primary interest is Heathen devotional work and she has both written and lectured extensively on this subject. Galina is heavily involved in the reconstruction of northern tradition shamanism and, in addition to several of her own books, has contributed extensively to Raven Kaldera's Northern Tradition Shamanism series. Galina holds a diploma in interfaith ministry from The New Seminary in NYC, a BA in religious studies from Empire State College and is currently pursuing her MA in religious studies at New York University. She is a member of the American Academy of Religion, the Religious Coalition for Reproductive Choice and a staff writer for NewWitch magazine. She may be reached at tamyris@earthlink.net.

> *Those who profess to favor freedom, yet deprecate agitation, are men who want crops without planting up the ground. They want the rain without thunder or lightening. They want the ocean without the awful roar of its many waters. The struggle may be a moral one; or it may be a physical one; or it may be both moral and physical; but it must be a struggle. Power concedes nothing without a demand. It never did and it never will.*
>
> *—Frederick Douglas*

Other Books by Galina Krasskova

Exploring the Northern Tradition (New Page Books)
The Whisperings of Woden (Booksurge Publishing)
Walking Toward Yggdrasil (Asphodel Press)
Sigdrifa's Prayer: An Exploration and Exegesis (Asphodel Press)
Full Fathom Five: A Devotional to the Norse Gods and Goddesses of
the Sea (Asphodel Press)

With Fuensanta Arismendi:
Root, Stone, and Bone: Honoring Andvari and the Vaettir of Money
(Forthcoming through Asphodel Press)

CPSIA information can be obtained at www.ICGtesting.com
Printed in the USA
LVOW13s0303270114

371096LV00001B/307/P